General editor	EVANGELIA KYPRAIOU
Text edited by	DIANA ZAFIROPOULOU
Design	VANA MARI
Translation	DAVID HARDY
Electronic processing of text	KATERINA ILIOPOULOU
Maps (p. 32, 37, 132)	IO GIANNELI
Colour separations	TOXON
Printing	EPIKOINONIA LTD

DIRECTION OF PUBLICATIONS - Panepistimiou 57, 105 64 Athens - www.tap.culture.gr

ISBN 960-214-278-2

Pylos - Pylia

A journey
through space and time

GEORGE PAPATHANASSOPOULOS - THANOS PAPATHANASSOPOULOS

PYLOS - PYLIA

A journey through space and time

NESTOR'S PYLOS

NAVARINO

METHONE

CORONE

For Konstantinos

Alexandros

Aspasia

PREFACE

According to the tales they used to tell, if you looked from a boat down into the depths of the sea in the bay of Navarino near Sphakteria when the light was right and the sea calm, you could see the masts of the Turkish and Egyptian ships sunk in the great naval battle of 1827.

If you happen to be at Old Navarino on a sunny winter's day, when there is exceptionally good visibility, and allow your gaze to wander over the sand-dunes of Voidokilia, Sphakteria, Niokastro, and Ai-Nikolas, and if you then turn towards the mountains of Kyparissia, Aigaleo, "a setting of majestic beauty, even by Greek standards", you cannot fail to feel yourself gripped by the pulse of History and Myth.

It was from here that Nestor set sail for Troy with the crews of his 90 ships, and later the Athenians fought the Spartans at Sphakteria for supremacy in the region. Romans, Avars, Franks, Genoese, Venetians, Spaniards from Navarre, Turks, Albanians and Egyptians have all set foot here as conquerors. The Ikonomidis brothers, Grigorios of Methone, Sachtouris, Makriyannis, and Santa Rosa fought here; so too did the admirals of Britain, France, and Russia, with their fleets.

In this same place they all mustered their troops, pitched camp, made their preparations, laid siege, defended themselves, erected fortifications, fought by land or sea, killed and were killed. So many dead in the one place. Bloody conflict was reenacted again and again, always with the same ferocity, for two and a half thousand years.

Neolithic, Early Helladic and Middle Helladic installations around the bay and in the surrounding area of Pylos, the palace of Nestor, the Hellenistic tombs and graves of Roman date at Divari, the Early Christian cemetery at Ayios Onouphrios, Paliokastro, Niokastro, the forts of Corone and Methone, the medieval aqueducts at Pylos, the church of Saint Leo at Paliomothoni – all these bear witness to the eternal dynamism of the geopolitical unit of south-west Messenia.

Bounded on the north by the Aigaleo range, this south-west corner of the Peloponnese has witnessed so many major historical events of both local and European importance that it may be justifiably be claimed that a significant part of Greek history has been played out here.

In "Pylos - Pylia", the most important monuments and significant historical events are set within the context of a more general process, and every effort has been made to avoid the disjointed character of a mere recitation of events.

Contemporary documents and texts are cited, as well as authentic accounts by the leading actors or eye-witnesses, in order to give clarity to the periods and historical events described and bring them to life. To make it easier for readers to comprehend some of the historical events and their consequences – at first sight of only local significance – there are frequent references to the circumstances and causes from which they sprang. It has been felt useful, for example, to give a picture of the grandeur and glory of Venice, the city that ruled the sea and dominated the Eastern Mediterranean for centuries, the city which played a decisive role in the fortunes of Methone, Corone, and Pylos.

Many of the illustrations are accompanied by extensive captions: these are designed as part of the text, which they accompany, supplement and enrich.

The fairly detailed chronological table was considered helpful as a quick reminder of the historical events, making this book a serviceable, easily understood "vade mecum".

The bibliography is organised according to subject, in an attempt to suggest the lines along which readers should be moving if they wish to read in greater depth about the history and exploration of the cities, regions and monuments mentioned in the text.

ACKNOWLEDGEMENTS

The authors wish to thank the Governing Board of the Archaeological Receipts Fund for including "Pylos - Pylia" in its publications list. Special thanks are due to the head of the Publications Direction, Evangelia Kypraiou, for her unstinting interest in the preparation of the book for publication, to Diana Zafiropoulou for the attentive editing and to Vana Mari for its design. We would also like to express our thanks to Professor Nikos Zias for recommending that "Pylos - Pylia" be included amongst the Archaeological Receipts Fund's publications.

Our thanks, too, to N. Karavias, the scholar and publisher from Pylos, for his assistance with the bibliography and his comments on topographical questions relating to the region; to the Director of the National and Historical Museum, Io. Mazarakis Ainian; to the archaeologist A. Solomou Prokopiou and to D. Koukiou Mitropoulou for their help in selecting the illustrations; also to the Gennadius Library and the American School of Classical Studies, especially E. Mitsou, M. Photiades, M. Voltera, N. Vogeikoff and to the Director of the Swedish Archaeological Institute, Berit Wells and her colleague Hilda Reit for their researches in the Nathan Valmin archives.

The authors would like to express their gratitude to the late Director of the Greek Institute of Venice, N. Panayiotakis, for permission to study in the Institute and for the hospitality he accorded them there; warm thanks also go to the architect N. Lianos for his assistance in tracking down evidence in the Venice archives in July 1987.

We extend grateful thanks to V. Konstantakopoulos for making the colour aerial photographs available. Thanks for other photographs go to Sp. Kourouniotis, T. Alexakis, G. Christophilopoulos, Ch. Androutsaki, who provided the photograph of the watercolour by Piet de Jong in her possession, to Tr. Sklavenitis, Researcher at the Centre of Modern Greek Studies for the photograph of Kostis Tsiklitiras, to D. Maravelias for his help in photographing the aqueduct of Pylos at the inaccessible site of Liakopoulo, and to the Byzantinist E. Stambogli for the letter in fig. 155. We thank T. Alexakis for the wide range of assistance that he provided throughout the study of the monuments of Pylos, the architect Chr. Kolliakou for the measured drawings and final presentation of the bastions at Corone, and E. Brousali and Io. Tsakiris for the final drafting of the maps of the south-west Peloponnese. Finally, we are grateful to Iord. Dimakopoulos for his valuable comments.

CONTENTS

The chapters dealing with the Mycenaean period were written by George A. Papathanassopoulos, and the other chapters by Thanos G. Papathanassopoulos. The preface, bibliography, and chronological table were composed jointly by the two authors.

Fig. 1. Pylos, with Niokastro in the background. The fortress is now surrounded by trees which would not have been present, when it was a functioning defence work.

SANDY PYLOS.
THE BAY OF NAVARINO

Navarino, the bay of Pylos, is the major geophysical feature of the Pylia region, and one of the largest natural harbours in the world, with a length of 4,800 m. and a width of 3,600 m. The sea in it reaches a depth of 50 m. The bay, facing the Ionian sea, is protected by the island of Sphakteria, which forms a huge natural breakwater. The island, now denuded of trees but forested in ancient times, is 4,000 m. long and varies in width from 500 to 1,000 m. At its highest point it rises to 150 m.

The bay of Navarino has two entrances: Megalo Perasma (Great Passage) at the south-west, which is 1,200 m. long and was formerly used by ships seeking to anchor in the calm waters of the bay, as it still is today; and the narrow, shallow opening of Sykia at the north, which is impassable to ships. Megalo Perasma, at the south end of Sphakteria, is dominated by the high, rocky islet of Tsichli-Baba, and in the middle of it there is a small, low rock called variously Chelonaki, Chelonisi, or Marathonisi. To the north of the bay

Fig. 2. The bay of Pylos.

Fig. 3. The bay of Pylos from the summit of Ai-Nikolas.

stretches the sandy coastal plain of Yialova and the lagoon of Divari. A short distance to the north-west, behind Divari, is another small bay called Voidokilia, which opens on to the Ionian sea.

The bay itself is dominated by two heights, Koryphasion at the north, overlooking Voidokilia, and Ai-Nikolas at the south, behind the modern town of Pylos.

Navarino, an ideal natural harbour and Homer's "sandy Pylos", lies on the sea route along the west coast of the Peloponnese. A harbour of this type, enjoying so many natural advantages, was naturally used from very early times.

Traces of the Neolithic period that have been identified in the so-called Cave of Nestor on Koryphasion, at nearby Voidokilia, and at other locations on hills in the surrounding area, attest to the presence of human beings as early as the middle of the 6th millennium BC. Finds from the nearby site known, after Pausanias, as the Tomb of Thrasymedes, demonstrate that there was a flourishing Early Helladic and Middle Helladic settlement here in the 3rd millennium BC.

The 2nd c. AD traveller Pausanias places Homer's Pylos at Koryphasion. He tells us that, "as they say", Nestor's house and tomb

Fig. 4. Koryphasion from the north. On the summit can be seen Paliokastro, with "Nestor's cave" below it.

Fig. 5. The "Tomb of Thrasymedes". The Mycenaean tholos tomb, which has been identified with the tomb of Nestor's son, occupies a dominating position at the north end of the Voidokilia bay. It was built at the centre of a Middle Helladic tumulus.

Fig. 6. *Small clay pyxis of the 12th c. BC, from Tragana. National Archaeological Museum, Athens.*

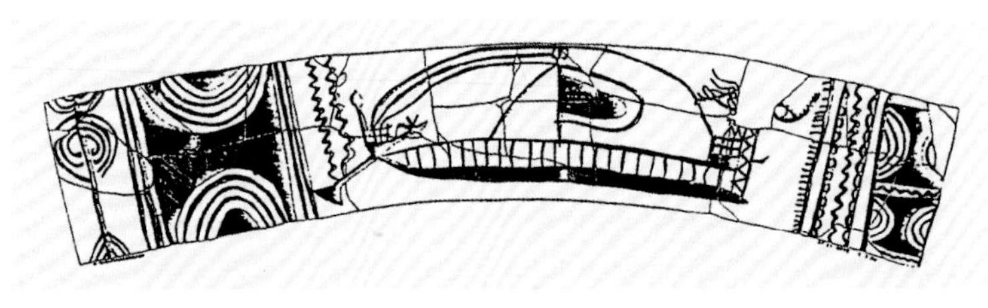

Fig. 7. Reconstruction drawing of the Mycenaean warship depicted on the pyxis in fig. 6.

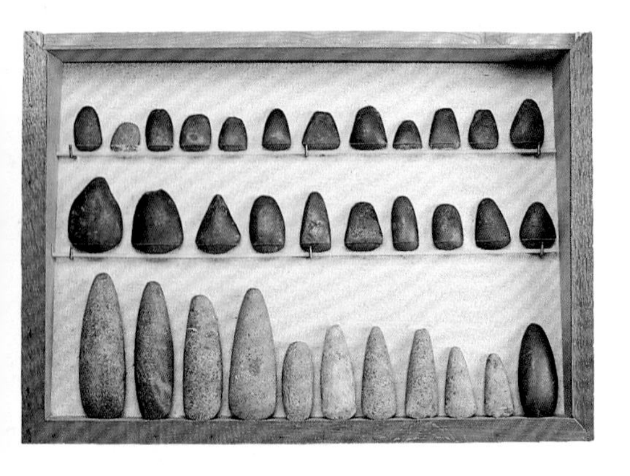

Fig. 8. Characteristic Neolithic tools-axes from Kotronakia near Chandrinou, to the east of the bay. Pylos Archaeological Museum.

were here, and close by was the "Tomb of Thrasymedes", one of his seven sons, and the cave where the Mycenaean king kept his oxen. Nestor's palace was discovered at Epano Englianos, 6 km. northwest of Koryphasion. The ruins of the palace, taken together with Homer's accounts, confirm that the kingdom of Nestor, extending as far as Mount Taygetos, was second only to Mycenae in power, prestige and wealth. Agamemnon, the leader of the panhellenic military expedition, sent one hundred ships to Troy; Nestor's contingent was ninety. Clearly the only place that the king of Pylos could have moored his ships was in the natural harbour. It was somewhere on the sandy beach of the bay, or in Voidokilia (the ancient Bouphras), that Telemachos, son of the king of Ithaca, Odysseus, disembarked on his visit to Nestor to discover why his father's return to his homeland was delayed.

Fig. 9. The small bay of Voidokilia between ancient Koryphasion (Paliokastro) and Divari.

THE MYCENAEAN CITADEL OF PYLOS

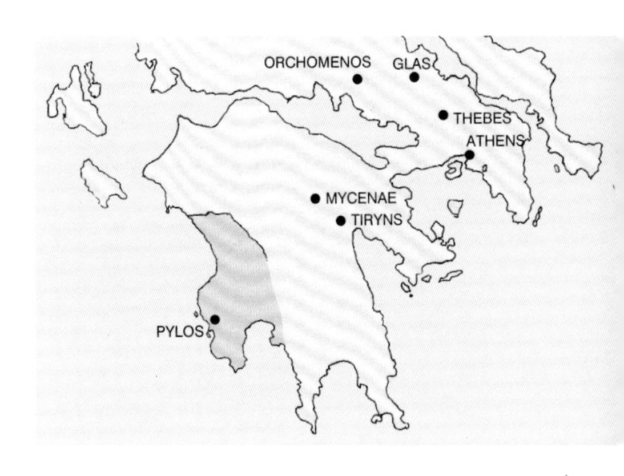

Fig. 10. The borders of Nestor's kingdom.

The noble, wise, sweet-speaking Mycenaean king Nestor, Homer's "horseman from Gerena", will have raised his eyes and gazed at his kingdom, "sandy Pylos", from his royal seat. Today, just as when Nestor ruled in the 13th c. BC, the hill of Epano Englianos that dominates the area, and over which extend the ruins of the largest known Mycenaean palace complex, affords a view of the rich land of Messenia with its endless olive-groves and vineyards.

From the coast to the soaring peaks of Messenian Aigaleo, which form the boundaries of the region, the land of Pylos governed by Nestor is a compound of grassy meadows and cultivated farms in the plains, low hills covered with heather, lentisks, holm-oaks, and arbutus, plane-trees and fern along the streams, and thyme, broom, and cyclamen in the hillsides.

It was here that Nestor's father, Neleus, son of Poseidon and Tyro, fled from Thessaly after quarrelling with his brother Pelias about who should succeed to the throne of Iolkos. Although it was founded by Pylos of Megara, the city of Pylos achieved such great prosperity and fame under Neleus that Homer refers to it as the city of Neleus.

Nestor, who ruled for three generations, could not see his entire kingdom from Epano Englianos, nor would he be able to see the

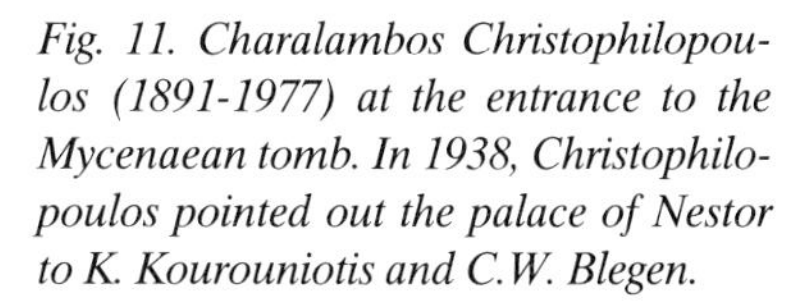

Fig. 11. Charalambos Christophilopoulos (1891-1977) at the entrance to the Mycenaean tomb. In 1938, Christophilopoulos pointed out the palace of Nestor to K. Kourouniotis and C.W. Blegen.

Fig. 12. Nionios Androutsakis (1920-1997) of Chora in Triphylia. Androutsakis was custodian of antiquities in Messenia and foreman of the major excavations and archaeological projects in the region.

Fig. 13. Photographed at Morosini's column: Tasos Diles (1924-1989), custodian of antiquities – the "soul" of the fortress of Methone, seated front; at the left is George Alexakis of Pylos (1918-1980), the craftsman who devoted his life to preserving and conserving the antiquities of Pylos.

Fig. 14. Carl William Blegen (1887-1971). The American archaeologist and Director of the American School of Classical Studies in Athens was a prolific excavator and author.

Fig. 15. Konstantinos Kourouniotis (1872-1945). Archaeologist and prolific writer who excavated in both Greece and Asia Minor. From 1920 onwards, he persistently searched for the Palace of Nestor at Pylos, and finally located it together with C.W. Blegen at Epano Englianos.

Fig. 16. Spyridon Marinatos (1901-1974). Archaeologist, scholar and investigator of Minoan and Mycenaean civilisation in many parts of the Greek world.

nine cities mentioned by Homer in the Catalogue of Ships (*Iliad* II, 591-596) as falling under his rule along with Pylos: *charming Arene* at Kato Samiko, *Thryon* on the Alpheios ford, well-built *Aipy* at Platiana, *Kyparisseeis* at modern Kyparissia, *Dorion*, at modern Malthi, and *Amphigenia*, *Pteleon* and *Elos*, the sites of which have not yet been identified.

Fig. 17. Reconstruction drawing of the Mycenaean palace complex of the Neleids.

The Greek archaeologists Andreas N. Skias and Konstantinos Kourouniotis, beginning in 1909 and 1912 respectively, located and investigated remains of Mycenaean date in Messenia in their search for the Mycenaean – Homeric – palace at Pylos.

Later, in 1938, Charalambos Christophilopoulos, a farmer from the nearby village of Koryphasion who was a lover of the ancient world, and to whom is due the discovery of almost all the important Mycenaean sites in Pylia and Triphylia, took Konstantinos Kourouniotis and his American colleague, Carl William Blegen, to Epano Englianos. The two archaeologists recognised the hill as "the most promising place" in which to conduct an excavation. The trial trenches dug by the two in the following year revealed important Mycenaean finds: well-built stone walls belonging to large rooms, fragments of wall-paintings, floors covered with durable plaster, Mycenaean pottery and tablets with Linear B inscriptions.

The palace of Nestor had been located and definitive evidence produced for the site of the seat of the Neleids. This had been placed by German Classicist Wilhelm Dörpfeld at Kakovatos in Eleia, where he had investigated a group of tholos tombs and the remains of a building complex.

Fig. 18. The Mycenaean citadel of Pylos with the earlier Palace of Neleus at the left and the Palace of Nestor at the right.
Palace architecture is the most brilliant achievement of the Mycenaeans. The palace was the residence of the king, and the political, military, administrative and economic centre of his kingdom. The largest and most important palaces are those at Mycenae, Tiryns, Athens, Glas in Boeotia, and Pylos.

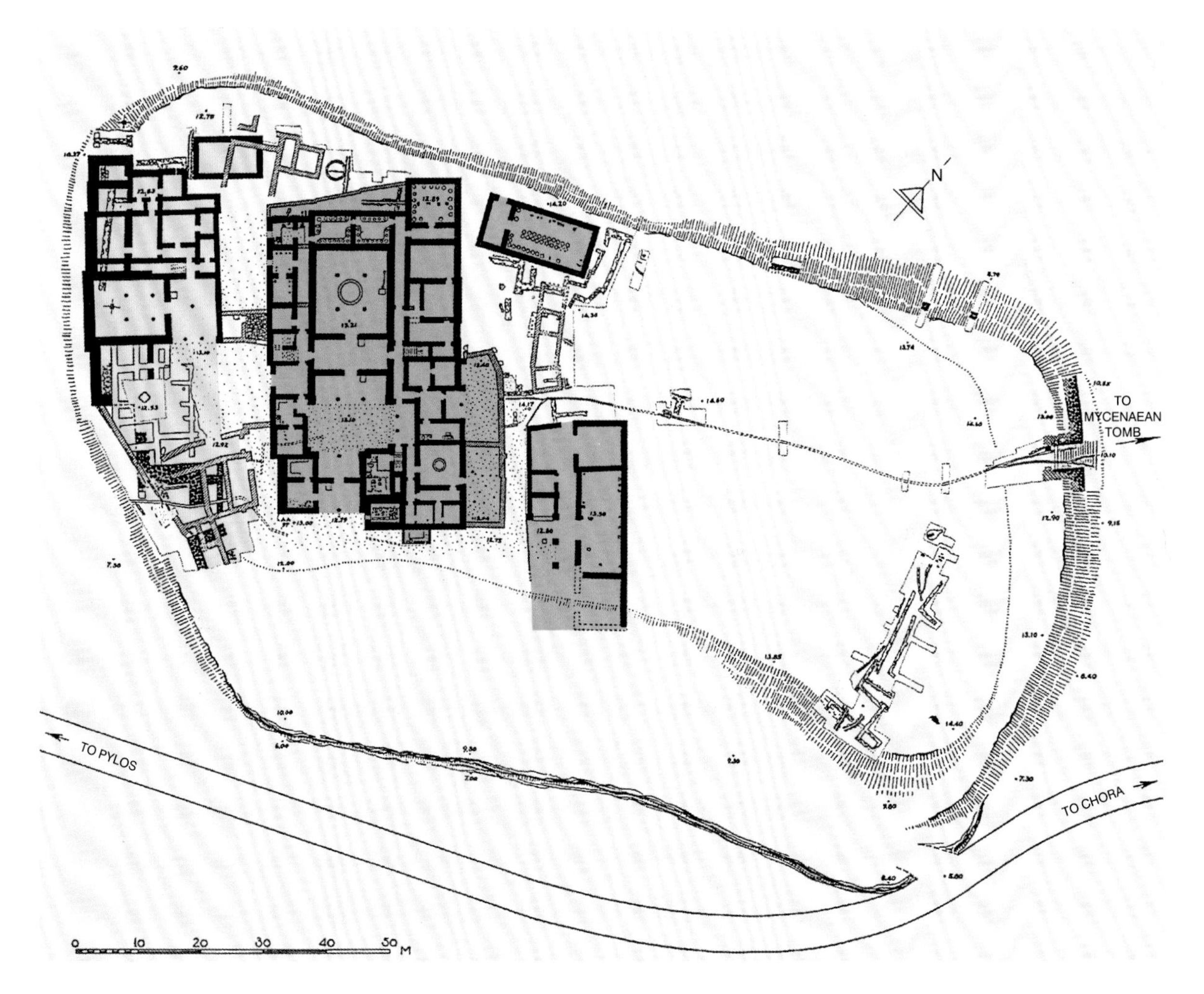

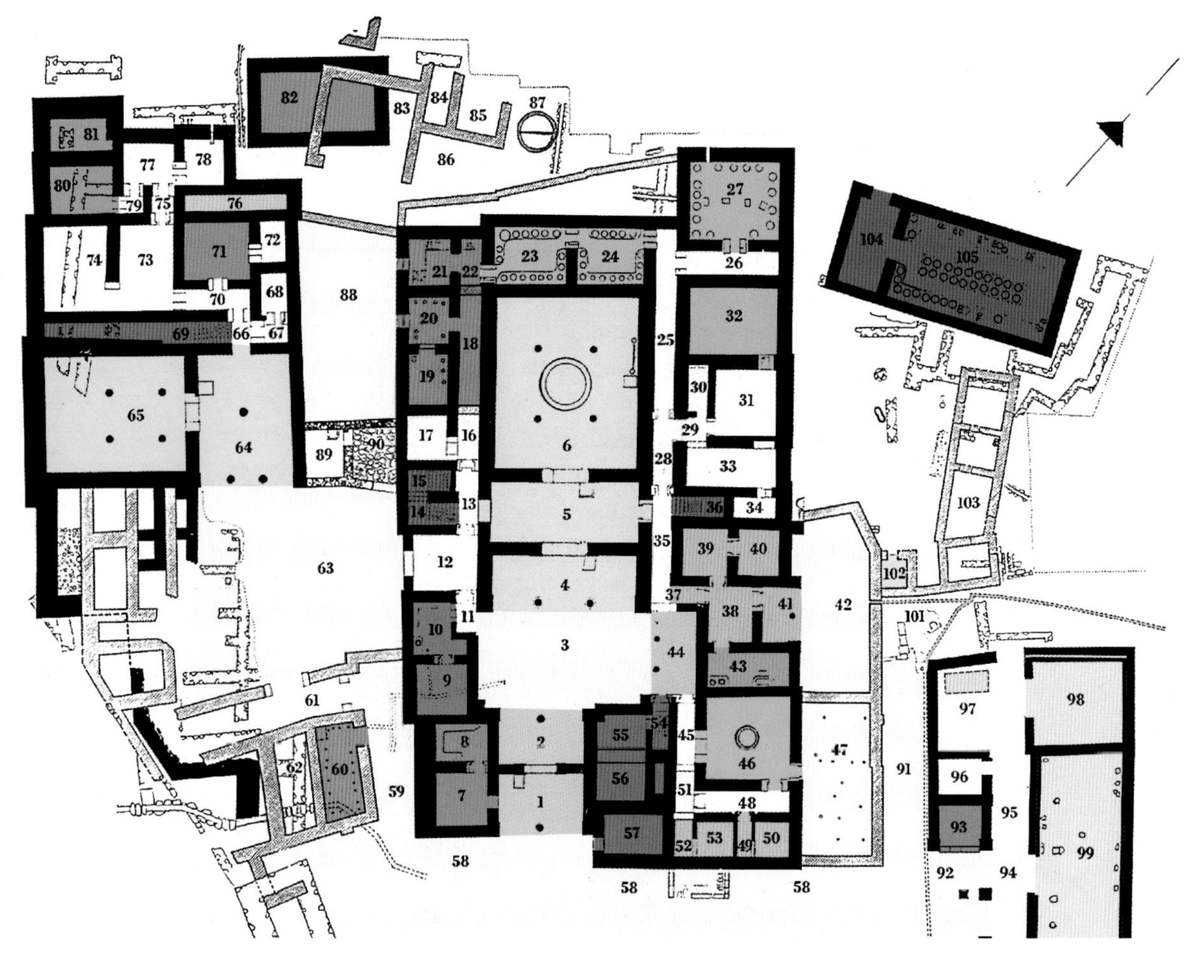

- PALACE RESIDENTIAL QUARTERS - MEGARON
- GARRISON
- OFFICERS' ROOM
- GUEST QUARTERS
- BATHROOM
- PROPYLON
- TABLET ARCHIVE
- BUFFET
- COURTYARD - ATRIUM
- OIL STOREROOM
- WINE MAGAZINE
- WINE OR OIL STOREROOM
- WAREHOUSE
- CORRIDOR (UNIDENTIFIED AREA)
- STAIRCASE
- TOILET
- LIGHTWELL
- WATCH TOWER
- CISTERN
- ::: AQUEDUCT
- SANCTUARY
- PALACE ARSENAL - WORKSHOP
- EARLY MYCENAEAN PIT GRAVE

Fig. 19. The palace complex at Pylos. The numbers are those assigned by the excavator. Different colours are used to indicate rooms and apartments that had an independent function and use, according to G.A. Papathanassopoulos.

It is beyond dispute, however, that the unique, well-preserved palace at Epano Englianos is the palace of Nestor, king of Pylos – the palace described by Homer in the third book of the *Odyssey* during his extensive account of the journey to Pylos of Telemachos, Odysseus's son, and his reception in the palace.

In the south-west part of the hill of Epano Englianos lie two independent building complexes on the acropolis which together constitute the brilliant complex of Mycenaean Pylos: the south-west building and the main building.

The south-west building has a total area of about 1,400 m^2, and lies close to the densely occupied part of the Lower Town. It is the earliest royal dwelling and is considered to be the palace of Neleus. The main building, with a total area of 2,000 m^2, is the palace of Nestor. It may be noted that the palace of Nestor is the best-preserved of all the Mycenaean palaces, with not only the foundations surviving but also the lower parts of the walls, in places up to a height of one metre.

Another structure on the acropolis, the north-east building, may have been an arsenal or a shrine, and there are two royal tombs a short distance away from the edge of the acropolis.

THE PALACE OF NELEUS

The most important and formal area in the palace complex of Neleus is a large room (65), with four or six columns supporting the roof, which is approached by way of an antechamber (64). This room was probably the earliest throne room. The antechamber had two columns on its open facade and a third placed irregularly, from a statics point of view, at its centre, at the point of intersection of the two axes of the three openings. The third column must, therefore, have been free-standing and did not reach the ceiling of the antechamber. This wooden free-standing column was visible from the court (63), the corridor (66), and above all from the most formal room in the palace (65), and will have had a religious character. The wooden columns of the antechamber and main room had closely set flutes, possibly as many as 44, and stood on stone bases. The formal character of room 65 has been confirmed by the discovery of traces of a hearth and the low structure designed for a guard to the right of the entrance. The two rooms will have had a splendid appearance, as is clear from the lavish frescoes that adorned their walls. Room 65 and antechamber 64 were the areas in which Neleus discharged his religious duties.

The palace of Neleus also included open and peristyle courts (63, 88), a large independent wine magazine (82), storerooms for food provisions (60, 67), a pottery storeroom (68), in which about 300 vases were discovered, most of them cooking vessels, a bathroom (78), corridors (61, 70), a staircase (69) leading to the upper storey, a lightwell (76), and a strong, imposing, two-storey, tower-like structure which had thick walls, judging from the massive foundations (81). The rooms of the complex were not laid out axially, but give a rather labyrinthine impression. The south-west side of the palace is 40 m. long, and consists of a continuous, thick, virtually straight wall that also functions as a retaining wall and separates the acropolis from the Lower Town. There is no entrance in this wall.

Fig. 20. Reconstruction drawing of a battle between the people of Pylos and the Arkadians (?) at a river, possibly the Iardanos. Fresco found in the vestibule (64) to the Throne Room of Neleus.

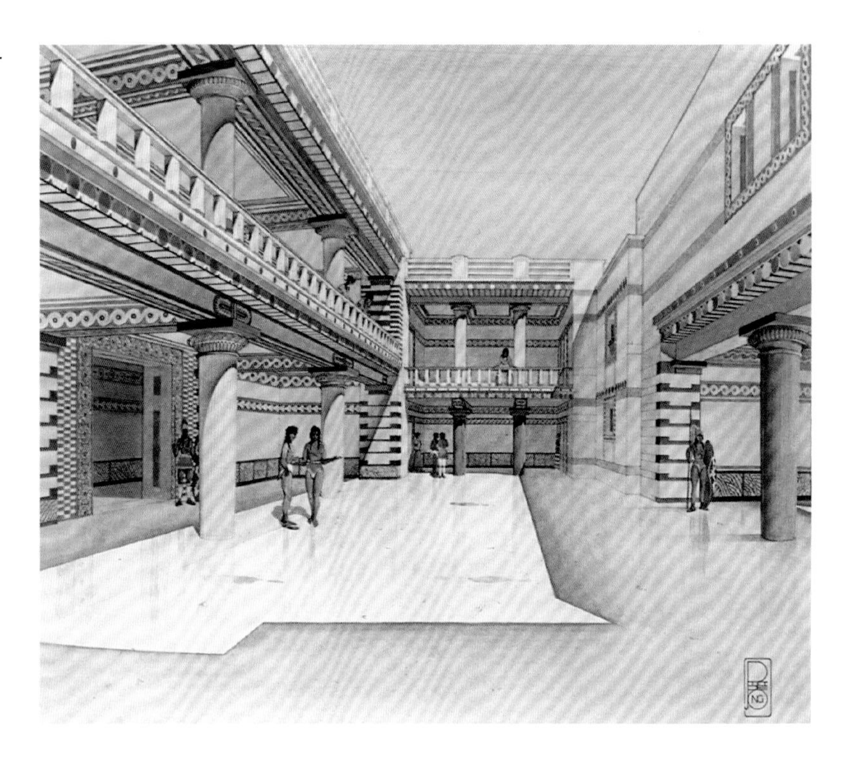

Fig. 21. Palace of Nestor. Reconstruction drawing of the atrium.

THE PALACE OF NESTOR

The palace of Nestor next to the palace of Neleus has a facade 30 m. wide and is 57 m. long, occupying the greater part of the entire building complex (1,900 m^2) on the hill. It is the best preserved of the palaces of the Mycenaean rulers discovered to date.

The palace is a compact building complex with a main court (3) and two open courts on the north-east side (42, 47), which are accessible only from within the palace. In addition to these it has fifty separate enclosed rooms of varying sizes and functions, above which there was an upper storey. Unlike the earlier palace of Neleus and the other contemporary Mycenaean palaces, the palace of Nestor is strictly rectangular in shape. It is developed symmetrically and harmoniously about a central axis and served predetermined needs. On the main axis are set, in order, the propylon (1, 2), the main court (3), and the megaron, with its portico (4), vestibule (5), and throne room (6).

The throne room, which measures 12.90 × 11.20 m., had a lavishly decorated floor, ceiling and walls, and was the core of the royal administration. It served as a room for receiving the leaders and representatives of other Mycenaean kingdoms, for gatherings and political negotiations, and for events of a religious, ritual, and cult nature, as well as for commercial exchanges that came within the competence of the king.

The floor of the throne room was covered with plaster divided into dense rows of squares which, apart from one painted with a fairly natu-

Fig. 22. Palace of Nestor. Reconstruction drawing of the Throne Room from the north-west, with the hearth at the centre. The prosperity and wealth of Nestor's kingdom are reflected in the grandeur of the palace, as attested by the numerous fragments of wall-paintings discovered during the excavations. These make it possible to arrive at a reliable restoration of the lavish decoration of the various areas.

ralistic rendering of a large octopus, were adorned with a range of linear motifs executed in red, blue, yellow, white, and black. The centre of the throne room is occupied by a large cult hearth, 4 m. in diameter and 20 cm. high, which was plastered and richly decorated. Four wooden columns, each with 32 flutes and standing on stone bases, were set symmetrically round the hearth and supported the upper storey and the high *opaion* (lantern), which admitted light into the room, making it sunny and pleasant, and also allowed smoke to escape. Between the hearth and the west column was found a stuccoed offering-table.

The throne was placed in the middle of the north-east side of the room, opposite the hearth. No trace has survived of the throne itself, which was probably made of wood decorated with ivory or some other inlaid material. Here, next to the position of the throne, was found a shallow hollow from which a V-shaped channel leads to another, somewhat lower hollow two metres away from the first. This structure was apparently used by the officiating king for libations to the gods, a ritual frequently mentioned in the Homeric poems.

Visitors, whether subjects or guests, will have been impressed by the enormous confronted griffins painted on the wall to right and left of the throne, with a lion, the guardian symbol of royal authority, behind them. The fresco of the lyre-player sitting on a rock, fragments of which were found in the east corner of the room, was painted to delight the Mycenaean ruler.

In the vestibule (5) to the throne room, and in the portico (4) con-

Fig. 23. Palace of Nestor. The hearth at the centre of the Throne Room.

tiguous with it, there were pedestals for the guards who controlled the entrance and protected the king. There was a similar pedestal at the outer propylon (1), which led into the inner propylon (2) and the court (3).

To right and left of the megaron are two narrow corridors, accessed from the vestibule (5) and the court (3). These led to ancillary and storage rooms on the ground floor and by way of two staircases up to the upper storey, which was presumably given over to the sleeping quarters of the royal family and more storerooms. The north-east corridor (37, 35, 28, 25) led to the upper storey by way of a staircase (36), and to an independent apartment consisting of six rooms (29, 30, 31, 32, 33, 34), the largest of which (32) was an oil storeroom. This same corridor led, by way of corridor 26, to the large northern oil storeroom (27). This was a later addition to the original palace structure, the plan of which had to be modified at this point to accommodate it. The corridor also led to two contiguous oil magazines (23, 24) behind the throne room, in which there were 33 pithoi fixed in a stucco bench.

Fig. 24. Palace of Nestor. Richly dressed aristocratic Mycenaean women, painted life size. From a fresco in corridor 51.

The corresponding south-west corridor (13, 16, 18, 22) also led to the upper storey by way of a staircase (14, 15), to the pottery storerooms (12, 17, 19, 20, 21, 22), and to the storerooms behind the throne room (23, 24). From this corridor, access could be had to two large courtyards (88, 63) that lay between the old and the new palace and secured communication between them.

At the north-east corner of the courtyard (3) is a hypostyle stoa (44) with two columns leading to three contiguous, though independent apartments:

a) the tower-like structure formed by rooms 55, 56, 57, the upper storey of which could be reached by a stone staircase (54);

b) the so-called queen's megaron (46), with a peristyle court (47), interior corridors and ancillary rooms (45, 51, 52, 48, 47); and

Fig. 25. Palace of Nestor. A griffin and a lion. From a fresco in room 46.

Fig. 26. Palace of Nestor. In the foreground is the oil magazine with the pithoi set in the ground (rooms 23 and 24) to the north-west of the Throne Room.

c) a central vestibule (38) which in turn led to two square, communicating rooms (39, 40) a bathroom (43) and a propylon (porch) (41) that opened on to a peristyle courtyard (42).

The excavator of the palace, Carl W. Blegen, considered that the tower-like structure (54-57), located at the palace propylon, was intended to be used as the headquarters of the palace garrison.

The second self-contained apartment, next to the garrison headquarters, was considered by the excavator to be a wing intended for the queen, comprising the queen's megaron (46), the queen's court (47), and the queen's private rooms (50, 53). The apartment is dominated by an elegant, almost square room (6.50 × 6.25 m.) with three entrances, known as the queen's megaron. The room has richly decorated walls and ceiling, and a hearth at the centre with similar decoration to that of the perceptibly larger hearth in the throne room.

It is hardly likely, however, that the queen's personal megaron with its private rooms and court would be built next to the garrison headquarters. The small hearth and the frescoes in the lavishly decorated room confirm the official nature of this area, but it is probably to be associated not with the queen, whose quarters will have been on the upper storey, but with the garrison commander and officers. The three doors in room 46, giving on to corridor 45, court 47, and another corridor that leads to the ancillary rooms (50, 51, 52, 53), provide support for the view that the area was much frequented and not, therefore, the personal apartment of the queen. Furthermore, if this wing were intended for the queen, it would imply that she exercised functions and competencies inconsistent with the period and for which there is no evidence in the Homeric poems.

The main feature of the third self-contained apartment is a small rectangular room (43) measuring 6.34 × 2.56 m., in which a terracot-

Fig. 27. Palace of Nestor. Bathroom (43). Decorated bathtub.

Fig. 28-29. Characteristic three-handled painted amphoras from various parts of the palace complex. Chora Archaeological Museum.

Fig. 30. Kylikes and other vases from room 20. Chora Archaeological Museum.
The hundreds of kylikes would have been arranged in roughly this fashion on the wooden shelves of the palace "bar".

ta bathtub with a richly decorated interior, and two water jars fixed in a bench are preserved *in situ*. The excavator considered this to be the royal bathroom.

Fig. 31. Male masks of gold and niello, from the embossed decoration of a silver bowl found near the palace entrance. National Archaeological Museum, Athens. Niello is a shiny black substance of metallic oxides, used as decoration in gold and silver ware.

Other self-contained areas in the main wing include a series of internally communicating two-room suites set along the left side of it.

One of these (19-20) and the three neighbouring rooms (18, 21, 22), which are behind the west corner of the throne room, formed the palace pottery storeroom. In it was found a total of 6,000 clay vases and household utensils of varying shapes, sizes and uses. These clay vases, which were kept on shelves and almost all of which were broken when found, served the needs of the palace, though some will certainly have been the object of trade.

Another two-room suite, consisting of the "bar" (9) and the waiting room (10), was to the left of the main court, from which there was an entrance to it. In the west corner of the waiting room is a bench with decorative painted plaster on which visitors to the palace sat and waited their turn to meet the ruler. Since they might apparently have to wait for some time, care was taken that wine was available, as may be concluded from the two pithoi found fixed in a bench in the south corner of the room, and the large number of kylikes on the floor of the adjoining room (9). These kylikes can now be seen in the floor, deformed and vitrified by the high temperature of the fire that caused the destruction of the palace.

The third self-contained two-room suite (7, 8) is at the entrance to the main palace complex, next to the outer propylon (1, 2).

The guard at the propylon seems to have controlled both the entrance to the palace and that to the two-room suite. In it were found about 1,000 tablets and fragments of tablets bearing Linear B inscriptions, confirming that this was the palace archives. An enormous pithos was found *in situ* in the south corner of the first room (7). Into this the subjects emptied the oil that they brought as tribute, after the quantities had first been recorded on the tablets. Three sides of the second room (8) had a plastered bench on which the tablets were apparently placed to dry after they had been inscribed, so that they could be classified and placed on the wooden shelves that ran around the walls of the room, one above the other.

In 1952 the British architect Michael Ventris succeeded after persistent efforts in deciphering the Linear B script, by studying the find from the palace at Pylos. Ventris's decipherment demonstrated that Linear B, which is also found at other Mycenaean centres, was the earliest written form of the Greek language. The Linear B tablets

Fig. 32. The huge oil pithos found in the archive (7). Chora Archaeological Museum.

Fig. 33. Michael Ventris (1922-1956). The English architect is famous for his decipherment of Linear B, in which he applied the methods of statistical analysis to the frequency with which the symbols occur on the tablets. In 1953, Ventris, in cooperation with the professor of linguistics J. Chadwick, published his seminal article "Evidence of Greek Dialect in the Mycenaean Archives" in JHS 73 (1953), p. 84-103.
After Ventris's untimely death, the unfinished task was continued by Chadwick, professor of linguistics at Cambridge University.

are possibly the most valuable find at the Mycenaean palace of Pylos, and it may be noted that the largest quantity of tablets was found here.

The study of the Linear B texts was initiated by Ventris, who was followed by Chadwick, and is continued by many scholars at the present day. It attempts to investigate the problem of the beginnings and evolution of written Greek in the Mycenaean period, before the use of the signs borrowed from the Phoenician alphabet became widespread in the first half of the 8th c. BC. The decipherment of Linear B was regarded as a major intellectual achievement, and one of the greatest successes of scholarship.

Fig. 34-35. The clay Linear B tablets Jn 829 and 641. No. Jn 829 is a list of contributions of bronze objects. No. 641 is known as the "tripod tablet". National Archaeological Museum, Athens.

Fig. 36. Drawing of the inscription on the "tripod tablet". The texts on the tablets date from the late 13th c. BC, and are mainly accounts records of the palace administration.

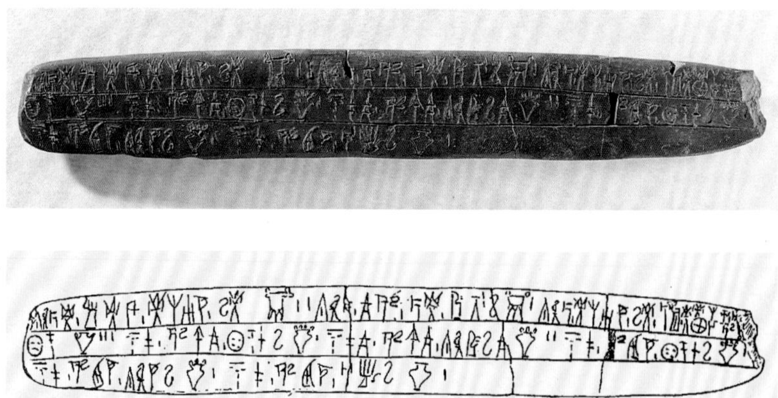

BUILDINGS TO THE NORTH-EAST OF THE PALACE

The large wine magazine

A large, free-standing, two-room building outside the limits of the palace, with an area of 250 m^2 (105), was the main wine magazine, or the royal wine cellar. It had a special antechamber for the official responsible for distributing the wine, which was kept in rows of pithoi along the sides of the large room, with a double row set on its main axis.

Fig. 37. Palace of Nestor. The large wine magazine (104-105).

The north-east building (arsenal - shrine)

The so-called north-east building is a large self-contained complex, also standing outside the palace limits. It consists of six rooms and a corridor, and probably a covered porch with a colonnade.

Three large rooms at the north-east of this complex (98, 99, 100) were apparently devoted to the manufacture and repair of metal and leather goods. About 100 Linear B tablets found here refer to repairs of leather and metal items, to supplies of bronze and leather, and to chariot equipment. This evidence, combined with the hundreds of weapon-tips, mainly arrowheads, found in rooms 98 and 100, indicates that the complex was a workshop producing military goods, and also the palace arsenal.

The most interesting room in the north-east building, however, is the small square room (93), which has an open front flanked by two bulky pilasters, and a rectangular stone altar in front of the entrance. One of the 100 inscribed tablets found in this room suggests that it was a shrine dedicated to Potnia Hippia, a goddess identified with Athena.

Fig. 38. Palace of Nestor. The north-east building from the south-east.

THE THOLOS TOMBS ON THE ACROPOLIS OF PYLOS

There are two royal tholos tombs near the palace complex. One of them, 145 m. from the palace at the south-east of the acropolis, had been looted and destroyed, and is preserved to a height of only 30 cm. Nevertheless, six undisturbed pit graves in its floor yielded, amongst other valuable finds, four large pithoi with a skeleton in each, 22 bronze swords and daggers, bronze vessels, and a large number of vases. No part of this tholos tomb is now visible, since the floor and pit graves were back-filled to protect them.

The other royal tholos tomb lies 90 m. from the gate of the acropolis, to the south-east (tholos tomb IV). It has a diameter of 9.35 m., dates from the 16th c. BC, and was used for successive burials possibly down to the 13th c. BC. The finds in this tomb, which was restored in 1957, included a gold seal with a depiction of a winged griffin (the royal emblem), four sealstones, a gold finger-ring with a depiction of a peak sanctuary of Minoan type, a large number of beads, most of them of amethyst, and four gold owls.

The numerous finds from the excavations by Blegen in the palace of Nestor, and the finds from the tholos tombs of Pylia and Triphylia excavated by Marinatos, which are now in the Archaeological Museum at Chora, Triphylia, give an excellent picture of the wealth and power of the Mycenaean world of Messenia.

Fig. 39. Palace of Nestor. Pit burials dug in the floor of the tholos tomb to the south-east of the acropolis.

Fig. 40-41. Palace of Nestor. Tholos tomb IV before and after the restoration of 1957.

THE END OF THE MYCENAEAN PERIOD AT PYLOS

In the late 13th or early 12th c. BC (LH IIIB or LH IIIC period), the Mycenaean palace at Pylos was comprehensively destroyed by fire, to which the close-set timber frames in the walls of the buildings made their contribution. The palace was subsequently abandoned and the site deserted. The destruction of the palace of Nestor and the destruction or burning of other contemporary palaces in Greece (Glas, Boeotian Orchomenos, the Kadmeion at Thebes, Mycenae, and Tiryns) were probably due to popular unrest and uprisings at the seats of the Mycenaean kingdoms, and were followed by widespread turmoil and political realignments.

After the destruction of the palace at Epano Englianos and the collapse of the central authority of the Mycenaean Neleids, life and culture continued unbroken at Pylos. This is reflected in following centuries both in the chamber and tholos tombs of Messenia, in which hero cults were practised in the Geometric and Archaic periods, and in the foundation and growth of a new city in the region. This city had the same name, Pylos, and was built on a coastal site at Koryphasion, overlooking the anchorage of Voidokilia.

Herodotus (V, 65) is of the view that the name of Peisistratos, the tyrant of Athens, goes back to a son of Nestor of this name.

The tradition that the Neleids ruled in Athens is also preserved by Pausanias (*Κορινθιακά* II, 18, 8-9). The traveller records that Thymoites, king of Athens who was descended from the line of Theseus, had to fight a duel with the Boeotian king Xanthos, who had laid claim to territories on the borders of Attica. Melanthos of Pylos, a descendant of Neleus and Nestor, offered to fight in place of Thymoites on condition that, if he were victorious, he would succeed him as king of Athens. Melanthos killed Xanthos and became king, introducing the foreign house of Neleus to royal authority at Athens. This probably accounts for the association between Athena, the patron goddess of Athens, and the owl, the symbol of the Neleids.

Fig. 42. Gold seal with a depiction of a winged griffin. From tholos tomb IV. National Archaeological Museum, Athens.

Fig. 43. Gold finger-ring from tholos tomb IV. National Archaeological Museum, Athens.

Fig. 44. Gold cutouts with embossed owls. From tholos tomb IV. National Archaeological Museum, Athens.

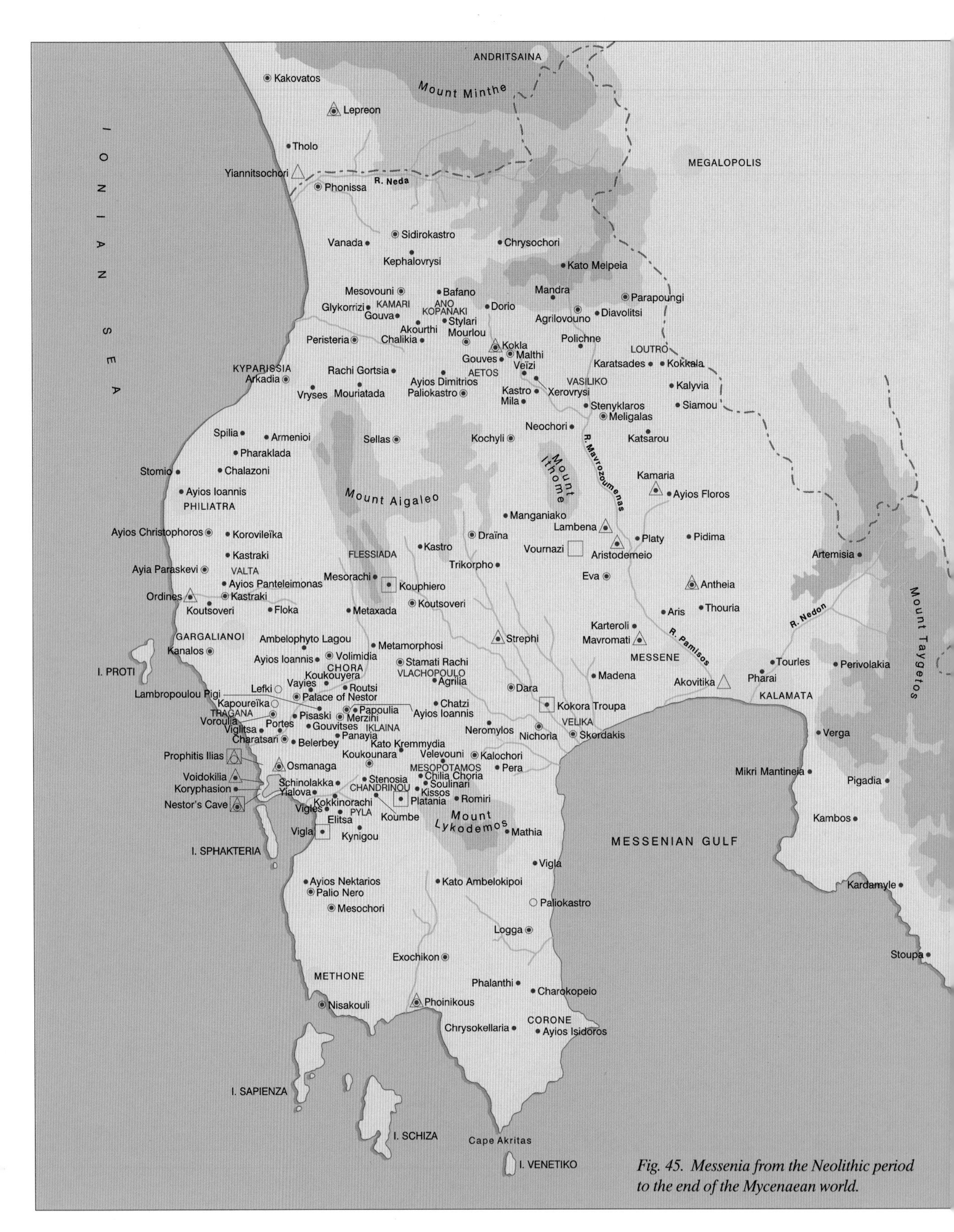

Fig. 45. Messenia from the Neolithic period to the end of the Mycenaean world.

□ LATE NEOLITHIC PERIOD (4800-3200 BC)

△ EARLY HELLADIC PERIOD (3200-2100 BC)

○ MIDDLE HELLADIC PERIOD (2100-1550 BC)

• LATE HELLADIC PERIOD (MYCENAEAN) (1550-1125 BC)

◉ Towns or townships, depending on the size of the population

The most common place-names of the area are given in CAPITALS

PYLOS FROM THE CLASSICAL PERIOD TO THE END OF ANTIQUITY

After the destruction of the palace of Nestor, Epano Englianos was abandoned and the centre of activity in the region shifted to Koryphasion, the hill to the north of the bay of Navarino, on which the new city of Pylos developed at some unknown date.

The myths and traditions associated with the bay of Pylos, which go back to the time of Nestor, were succeeded by the important historical events played out in Messenia, which led to the subjection of Pylos and the entire area to the Spartans as a result of the three Messenian Wars (743-724, 685-667, and 464-454).

Later, in 425 BC, Pylos found itself once more on the stage of history during the Peloponnesian War. In the seventh year of the war the Athenians sent 40 ships to Sicily under the generals Sophokles and Eurymedon. As they sailed around the Peloponnese, the ships were

Fig. 46. Bronze shield bearing the dotted inscription: ΑΘΗΝΑΙΟΙ ΑΠΟ ΛΑΚΕ-ΔΑΙΜΟΝΙΩΝ ΕΚ ΠΥΛΟ (The Athenians from the Spartans at Pylos). Ancient Agora Museum, Athens.
The shield was found in the Athenian Agora. Pausanias states that the Athenians hung the shields of the Spartans taken prisoner on Sphakteria in the Stoa Poikile (I, 15, 4). The shield illustrated here is presumably one of them.
To commemorate their victory at Sphakteria, the Athenians dedicated a bronze statue of Athena Nike on the Citadel (Pausanias, IV, 36, 6-7).

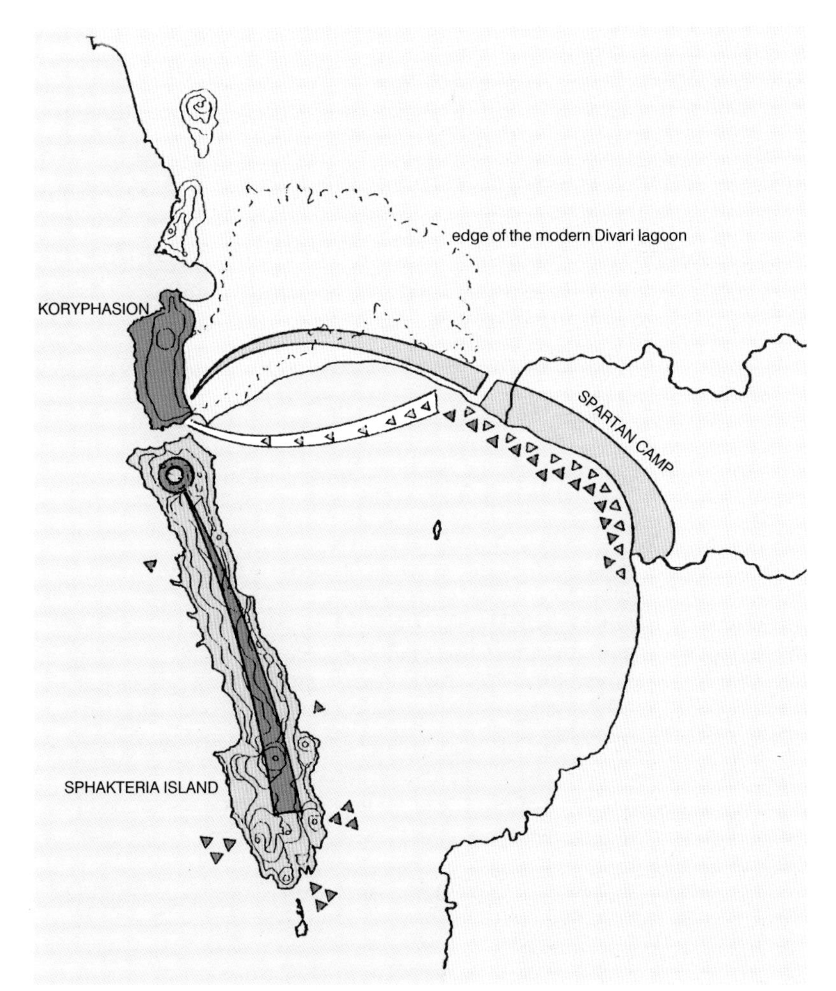

Fig. 47. The bay of Pylos. The disposition of the Spartan and Athenian forces at the battle of Sphakteria in 425 BC.

SPARTANS
ATHENIANS
FINAL BATTLE
SPARTANS TAKEN PRISONER
UNSUCCESSFUL SPARTAN ASSAULT
ON KORYPHASION BY LAND AND SEA
CLASHES OF THE RIVAL FLEETS
ATHENIAN ADVANCE TO SPHAKTERIA

Fig. 48. Thucydides (460-396 BC). Roman marble copy of a 4th c. BC bust of the Athenian historian. National Museum of Naples.

compelled by a storm to seek shelter in the great bay. The experienced general Demosthenes was accompanying the expedition with a special assignment to use the fleet as he judged best on its voyage around the Peloponnese. Demosthenes realised the advantages of the area and persuaded the Athenians to fortify Koryphasion, on which stood Pylos, a hamlet abandoned at some unknown date. His aim was to create an Athenian naval base on Lacedaemonian territory from which the Athenians and Messenians would be able to harass their long-standing enemy. Having erected fortifications on Koryphasion within six days, Demosthenes stayed at Pylos with five ships and sent two to Athens to request reinforcements, while the rest of the fleet went on to Sicily.

The Spartans were alarmed and ordered their army, which had invaded and was devastating Attica under king Agis, to desist from this activity and proceed to Pylos. They also recalled their fleet of 60 ships from Corcyra for the same purpose. When the Spartan army and fleet arrived at Pylos, the hoplites encamped at the head of the bay, with the fleet before them. To prevent the Athenians from using Sphakteria as a base, a crack Spartan corps landed on the island and fortified it, at the same time launching an attack on Demosthenes' fortress on Koryphasion.

The Spartan attack by land and sea was repulsed by the 600 men with Demosthenes. During the battle the Spartan general Brasidas, who had prevented the Athenians from founding a military base at Methone six years earlier, was wounded and lost his shield. The shield was found by the Athenians who used it later in the trophy they set up to commemorate their victory.

Thucydides, who devotes the first forty chapters of Book IV to the clashes between the Athenians and Spartans at Pylos, gives the following picture of the dramatic scenes of the final battle on Sphakteria:

"[The Spartans] were thrown into consternation by the shouting which accompanied the attacks; great clouds of dust rose from the ashes where the wood had been recently burned, and what with the arrows and stones loosed from so many hands and flying through the dust-cloud, it became impossible to see in front of one. Things now began to go hard with the Spartans; their felt helmets could not keep out the arrows; when they were hit with spears the broken shafts stuck in their armour, and they themselves, unable to see what was in front of them, had no means of fighting back; words of command were inaudible, being drowned by the shouting of the enemy; danger was on every side, and they could see no possible way either of defending themselves or of escaping".

(Thucydides, IV, 34, translated by Rex Warner, Penguin edition)

Fig. 49. The Nike of Paionios. After the victory at Pylos, the Messenians and Naupaktians, who fought with the Athenians, dedicated to Zeus a brilliant statue of Nike (Victory) by the sculptor Paionios of Mende in the Chalkidike. Museum of Ancient Olympia.

The 50 Athenian ships sent as reinforcements did not put in at Pylos but anchored for the night off the island of Prote. On the morning of the following day they sailed into the bay using both entrances and clashed with the Spartan fleet, emerging victorious. The Athenian enthusiasm at this victory was so great that they pursued the enemy ships towards the coast, tied them to their own ships and pulled them off, while the Spartans leapt into the sea fully armed and tried to hold them back. Thucydides was impressed by the paradox that occurred in the bay of Pylos, with the Athenians fighting a land battle from ships and the Spartans waging a naval conflict from dry land. The result was that not only did the Spartans fail to capture the enemy fort on Koryphasion, but their force on Sphakteria was cut off by the Athenians who mounted frequent naval patrols around the islet.

The events at Pylos became the focus of the war. The Athenian Kleon had been elected hellenotamias in 427 BC and had also had the office of general bestowed upon him by the popular assembly. As soon as he found that the Athenians were intending to land on Sphakteria he went to Pylos to lead the operation himself. Peace negotiations designed to secure the rescue of the Spartans cut off on the islet began but led nowhere. The Athenians then landed on Sphakteria where, after fierce fighting, the 292 Spartans who survived were obliged to surrender, having defended themselves for 72 days. The Spartan prisoners-of-war were taken to Athens, and their liberation became a Spartan condition in negotiations during the rest of the war. This capture of the Spartans was regarded as a serious humiliation for Sparta, since it was the first defeat she had ever suffered on her own territory.

After defeating the Spartans on Sphakteria, the Athenians left a permanent garrison at Pylos, which was reinforced by Messenians, and Demosthenes' fort thus became a strong military base.

When the peace of Nikias was concluded in 421 BC, the Athenians set free the Spartans prisoner-of-war captured on Sphakteria, but retained their fortified base at Pylos. After the renewal of hostilities, the Lacedaemonians successfully besieged the Athenian fort and captured the site in 409 BC. Pylos was once more abandoned.

Demosthenes, who played a leading role in the military events at Pylos, was put to death by the Syracusans in 413 BC, along with Nikias, during the disastrous Athenian expedition to Sicily.

Pylos recovered its position as a Messenian port in 369 BC, after the victories of Epaminondas over the Spartans, which led to the liberation of all the Messenian helots and the foundation of the city of Messene. Nevertheless, the lack of any strong political figure in Messenia and the

Fig. 50. Strigils from burials of athletes in the Tsopani Rachi tumulus. Pylos Archaeological Museum.
Athletes used strigils to scrape oil and mud from their bodies after an athletic contest.

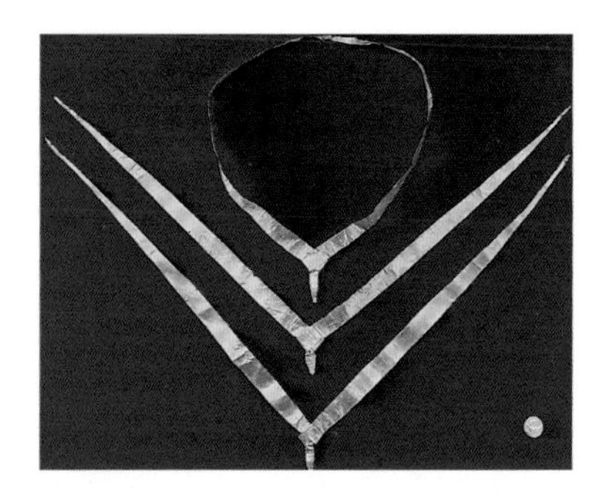

Fig. 51. Gold diadems from tombs of athletes in the Hellenistic tumulus at Tsopani Rachi. Pylos Archaeological Museum.

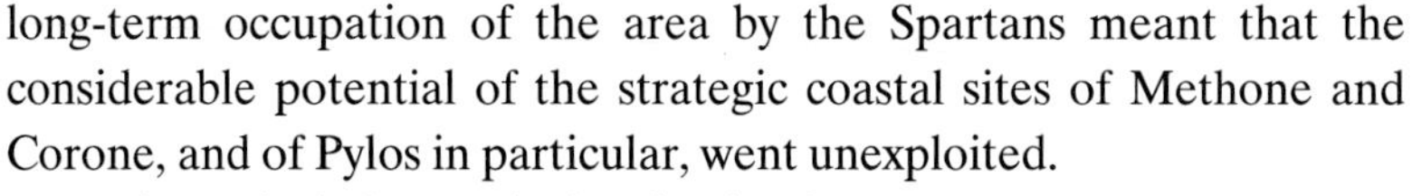

long-term occupation of the area by the Spartans meant that the considerable potential of the strategic coastal sites of Methone and Corone, and of Pylos in particular, went unexploited.

In the period of Macedonian domination of Greece Pylos is recorded as a free Messenian city, a status it continued to enjoy in the Hellenistic and Roman periods; this is evident from the ancient cemetery at Divari, from the dates of the coins issued by Pylos, and from Pausanias's account, according to which he saw not only the house of Nestor and the Tomb of Thrasymedes, but also the cave in which the Mycenaean king kept his oxen, and a sanctuary of Athena Koryphasia (*Μεσσηνιακά* IV, 36, 2).

To the east of Koryphasion lies Divari, a lagoon which seems from the archaeological record to have begun to form after Roman times, when the sea level rose by 1.50 m. An extensive Hellenistic cemetery discovered here attests to the prosperity of Pylos at this period. Further confirmation for the city's flowering is provided by the Hellenistic burial mound for athletes found at Tsopani Rachi between ancient Pylos at Koryphasion and the ancient city of Erana further to the north. This Hellenistic mound has yielded gold diadems, silver coins, bronze strigils, hundreds of clay vases and vessels, and excellent quality glass vases, including a *millefiori* skyphos.

In the Hellenistic period, Pylos was a member of the Achaian League (219 BC), and in Roman times issued its own coinage.

Virtually nothing is known of Pylos for the period of ten centuries that followed the end of the Roman empire, for which there are no monuments, literary sources, or archaeological finds.

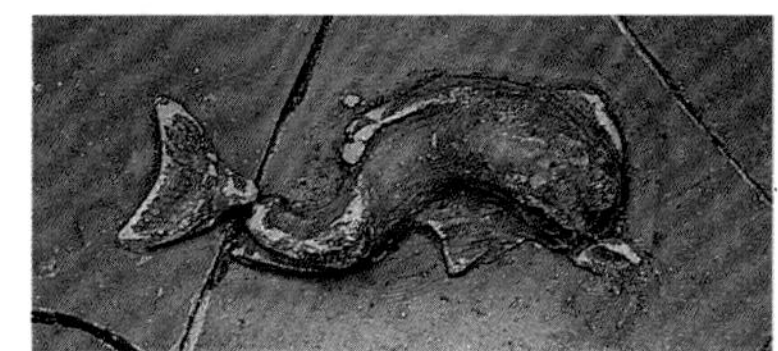

Fig. 52-53. Clay black-glaze skyphos from the Tsopani Rachi tumulus. There is a relief dolphin on the well and the relief figures from a Dionysiac scene on the exterior. Pylos Archaeological Museum.

Fig. 54-56. Glass skyphoi from the athletes' tumulus at Tsopani Rachi. Pylos Archaeological Museum. The skyphos in fig. 55 is of "millefiori type", a rare glass technique developed in the Hellenistic period.

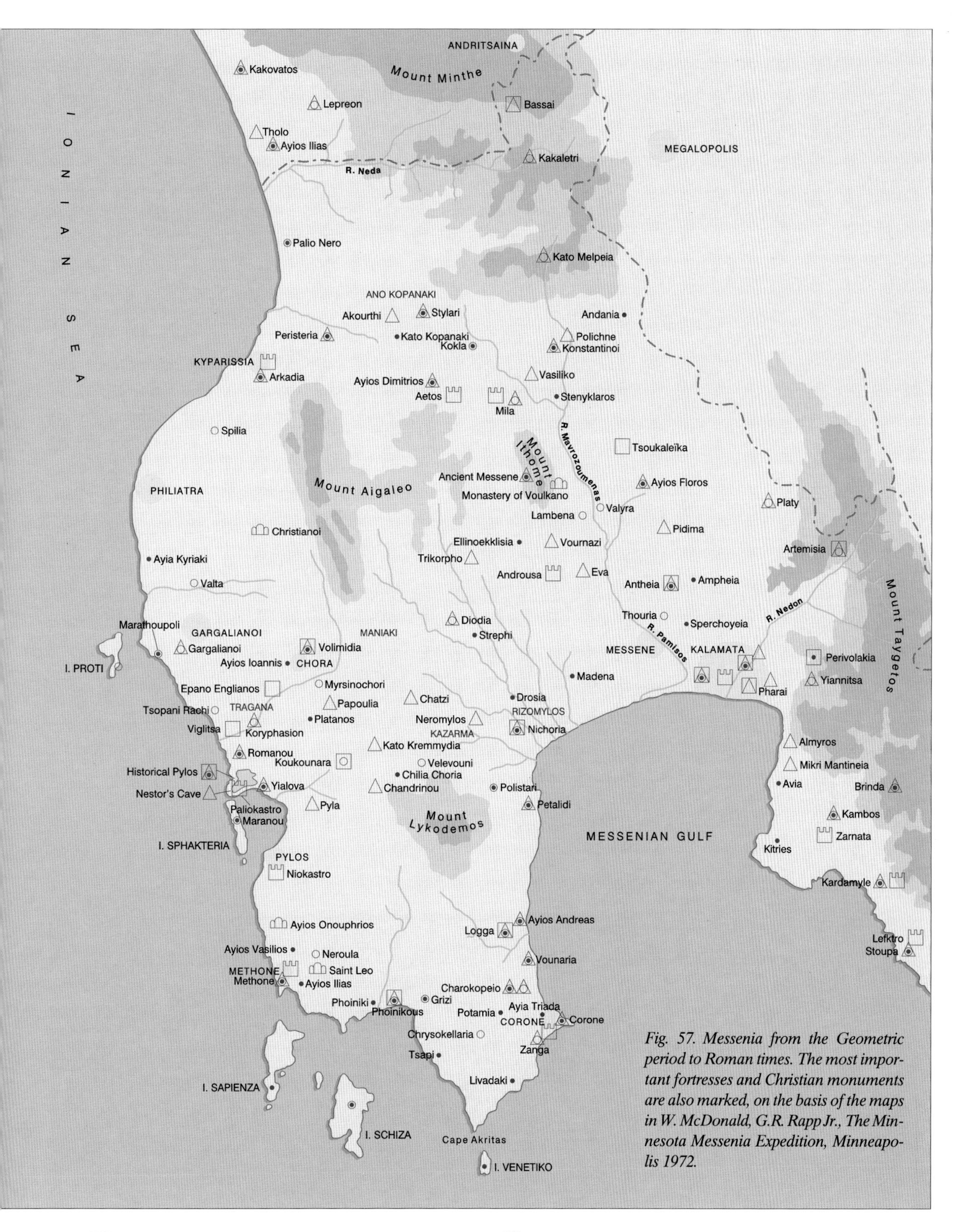

Fig. 57. Messenia from the Geometric period to Roman times. The most important fortresses and Christian monuments are also marked, on the basis of the maps in W. McDonald, G.R. Rapp Jr., The Minnesota Messenia Expedition, Minneapolis 1972.

□ PROTOGEOMETRIC-GEOMETRIC PERIOD (1125?-700 BC)
△ ARCHAIC-CLASSICAL PERIOD (700-360 BC)
○ HELLENISTIC PERIOD (360-31 BC)
• PERIOD OF ROMAN DOMINATION (31 BC-AD 330)

MEDIEVAL FORTRESSES
CHRISTIAN MONUMENTS
Towns or townships, depending on the size of the population

The most common place-names of the area are given in CAPITALS

FRANKS, VENETIANS, AND TURKS

In the early years of the 13th c. AD two events set their stamp on world history. In the East, the Mongols swept through Asia under Ghengis Khan, their progress culminating in the conquest of China in 1206. In the West, two years earlier in 1204, the Franks captured Constantinople during the Fourth Crusade, an event that led to the dismemberment of the Byzantine empire over a period of about half a century.

Hostility between the Greeks of Byzantium and the Western Europeans, which can be discerned as early as the Second Crusade (1147-1149), in combination with the commercial ambitions of the Venetians, led to the capture and pillaging of Constantinople by Frankish knights, who arrived in Venetian ships to take the brilliant city. A detailed description of the siege and capture is given by Geoffrey Villehardouin, one of the leaders of the Fourth Crusade. Villehardouin tells us that "never before, since the foundation of the world, was so much booty taken from a single city." (Geoffrey Villehardouin, *The Conquest of Constantinople*, London 1829, § 250). For 57 years after this date, the emperor in Constantinople was a Frank. The Byzantine central authority was dissolved and the Greek territories were distributed amongst European knights; earldoms, baronies, duchies and principates were created on the model of Western European institutions. The period from 1204 to 1430 in Greece is accordingly known as the Frankish period.

The Franks ceded three eighths of Byzantine territories to the Venetians. The latter gradually extended their jurisdiction not only to Methone and Corone, but also to the Ionian islands, the Cyclades, and Crete, followed later by Cyprus (1489); in the 15th c., The *Serenissima Repubblica* of Venice was not only mistress of the eastern Mediterranean Sea, but also the centre of world trade.

When Venice was unable to establish new peaceful commercial relations

Fig. 58. The capture of Constantinople by the Franks.

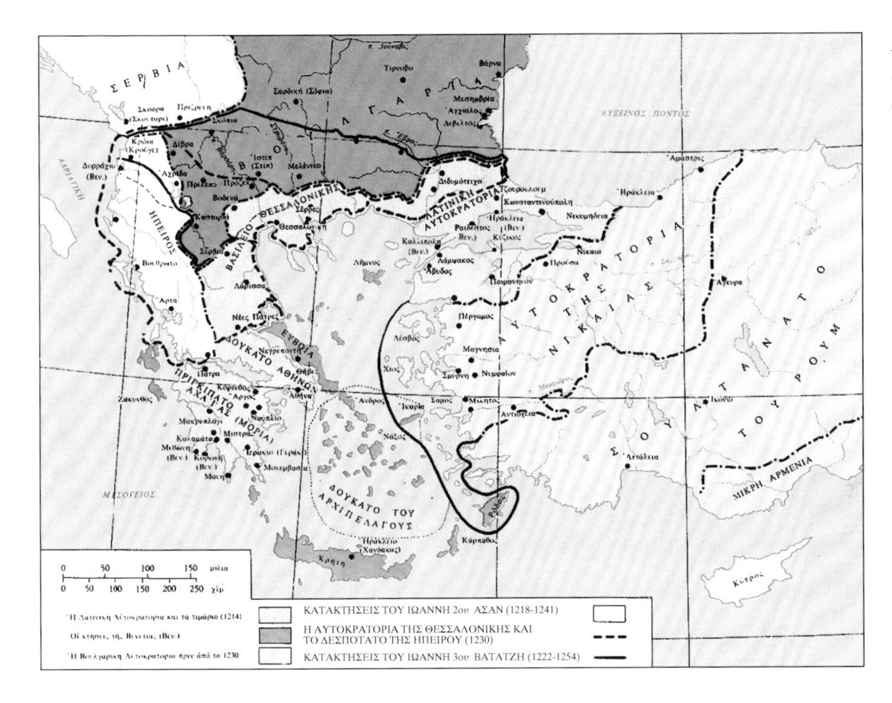

Fig. 59. The regions of the Byzantine empire conquered by the Franks and Venetians (1204-1261).

with the Turks or preserve the privileges essential to the movement of goods, she was prepared to fight fiercely and relentlessly to secure her trading posts on the sea lanes. The centuries that followed were marked by a succession of wars between the Venetians and Turks, which continually spread to Greek lands. In this way, the *Serenissima Repubblica* gradually lost Chalkis and the whole of Euboea (1479), Naupaktos (1499), Navarino, Methone and Corone (1500), Nauplion and Monemvasia (1540), Chios (1566), Cyprus as a result of the sieges of Nicosia (1570) and Famagusta (1571), Chania (1645) and the whole of Crete after the siege of Herakleion, which lasted twenty-five years (1645-1669). The Turks failed only to extend their rule to the Ionian islands, with the exception of Lefkas, which they held for a few decades (1684-1744).

In the Peloponnese, the Franks established themselves on the west coast, where they created the Principate of Achaia, or Principate of the Morea, using the old forts and fortified sites of the Byzantines to protect the conquered territory. The Franks reinforced the fortresses at Akrokorinthos, Argos, Kalamata, Nauplion, Kyparissia, and Patra, and erected new castles at Chlemoutsi (castel Tornese), the bay of Navarino, Mystras, Karytaina, and Passavas.

The Greeks returned to power in 1261, when Michael VIII Palaiologos became emperor at Constantinople. The Byzantine empire, however, never recovered from the devastating blow inflicted on it by the Europeans. Already enfeebled, it was finally extinguished by the Turkish conquest two centuries later in 1453.

In 1430, Thomas Palaiologos, brother of the last emperor of Constantinople, Konstantinos XI Palaiologos Dragasis, dissolved the Frankish Principate of Achaia and overthrew its last ruler, Centurione II Zaccaria. The Greeks once more became masters of the Peloponnese, apart from Methone, Corone, Nauplion, and Argos, which remained in Venetian hands.

Fig. 60. Old map of the Peloponnese (1684) by the Dutch geographer F. de Witt. The three sides are bordered by depictions of the fourteen coastal fortresses captured by Morosini during his campaign.

Dates of capture of the fortresses (from the top left):

S. MAURA (Lefkas)	*6 August 1684*
CORON (Corone)	*11 August 1685*
ZARNATA (Zarnata)	*11 September 1685*
NAVARINO (Niokastro)	*18 June 1686*
MODON (Methone)	*10 July 1686*
NAPOLI DI ROMANIA (Nauplion)	*3 September 1686*
PATRASSO (Patra)	*24 July 1687*
LEPANTO (Naupaktos)	*25 July 1687*
CORINTO (Akrokorinthos)	*1 August 1687*
CAS. TORNEZE (Chlemoutsi)	*3 August 1687*
MISTRA olim SPARTA (Mystras)	*27 August 1687*
ATENE (Athenian Citadel)	*29 September 1687*
MALVASIA (Monemvasia)	*12 August 1690*

CERIGO (Kythera) Venetian possession since the beginning of the 13th c.

Built on the Adriatic marshes, the "floating city", with its powerful navy and many conquered territories, mainly in the Aegean and Ionian seas, was for centuries the dominant trading and naval power in the Mediterranean. It was mainly the Venetians who were responsible for diverting the Fourth Crusade from the Holy Land to Constantinople; in the distribution of Greek territories that followed, Venice received Crete, Euboea, some of the Aegean islands, and part of the Peloponnese.

In the 15th c., Venice was the leader of world trade and had developed its own network of colonies in the Adriatic, Ionian, Aegean and the Black Seas. Methone and Corone were ports of call on the way from the East to the West and vice versa. The decline of Venice in the 18th c. was completed in 1797, when it was captured by Napoleon. The city was finally annexed to the newly founded kingdom of Italy.

The capture of Constantinople by the Turks in the middle of the 15th c. ushered in a period of historic changes. Hopes that Turkish expansionism would be checked by the united Christian powers of Europe proved illusory, the use of firearms became widespread, the Hundred Years' War between France and England came to an end, nation states began to form in Western Europe, and the great voyages of discovery began. The Middle Ages were entering upon their twilight and the portents of the Renaissance could be heard.

The expansion of the conquering Ottoman empire in the 17th c. reached its climax in 1683 when the Turks reached the city of Vienna, to which they laid siege. The Turkish failure to capture the Habsburg capital in this second siege (the first, which also failed, was in 1529) marked the beginning of the gradual decline of the Ottoman empire.

The Venetians, who had never ceased to covet their old bases in Greece, especially after the loss of Crete, decided to return and resume the war with the Turks. In 1684, under the general leadership of Doge Francesco Morosini and using Lefkas and Preveza as their bases, they initiated a campaign of conquest in Greece and by 1687 had captured all the coastal forts in the Peloponnese apart from Monemvasia.

In June 1686, the Venetians landed 10,000 infantry and 1,000 cavalry at Navarino. The Turkish garrison of Paliokastro surrendered to the leader of the Venetian land forces, the Swede Otto Königsmark, a veteran of the Thirty Years' War (1618-1648). The following month, the Venetians laid siege to Niokastro, which held out for only twelve days before surrendering, after a close siege by land and sea.

By 1687 the Venetians had made themselves masters of Athens and Chalkis; famously, it was during this capture of Athens that the Parthenon, the supreme monument of mankind, was blown up as a result of the Venetian bombardment.

Fig. 61. The doge of Venice, Francesco Morosini (1618-1694), who was known as Peloponnisiacus. Before he became doge in 1688, Morosini was Admiral of the Venetian fleet.

Fig. 62. Venice. The palace of the doges and the Grand Canal.

Fig. 63. The bay of Navarino and the operations to capture the fortress in July 1686.

After Morosini's successful campaign, the Venetians divided the Peloponnese into four *territori*: that of Romania, with its capital at Nauplion *(Napoli di Romania)*, Achaia, with its capital at Patra *(Patrasso)*, Lakonia, with its capital at Monemvasia *(Malvasia)*, and Messenia, with its capital at Niokastro *(Navarino Nuovo)*. *Provveditori* (overseers) were installed in the capitals of the provincial *territori*, with a general *provveditore* at Nauplion. The *territore* of Messenia included not only Methone, Corone, Androusa, Kalamata, and Kyparissia, but also part of Arkadia as far as Leontari, Phanari, and Karytaina.

The written reports sent by the *provveditori* to the Council of the Doges, and the instructions sent by the latter relating to all matters of concern in the Venetian *territori*, have preserved valuable evidence for the situation in the Peloponnese at this period.

In 1715 the Sultan Ahmet III assigned the task of recovering the Peloponnese to the Grand Vizier Ali Kioumourtzi who, in a lightening campaign, drove the Venetians from the fortresses and restored Turkish rule. This brought to an end what is known as the Second Venetian period in Greece, which lasted for thirty years – the final fifteen of the 17th and the first fifteen of the 18th century.

The Second Venetian period was a Christian parenthesis in the Turkish occupation of Greece. Not only did it disappoint the hopes of the enslaved Greeks yet again, who anticipated that a Christian power opposed to the Ottoman Turks would assist them, but converted these hopes into terrible memories, for the Venetian conquerors were frequently just as harsh as the Turkish rulers.

PALIOKASTRO AT ANCIENT KORYPHASION

From Didymoteicho to Rhodes and from Phokaia to Preveza, all the castles have the same character, as though they were made by the same master craftsman, appointed by the same castellan.

(Ph. Kondoglou, *Ταξείδια*, Athens 1928)

After the Early Christian cemetery of Ayios Onouphrios at Methone and the fortresses dating from the early 13th c. at Methone and Corone, the most important building remains attesting to the history of the area are those of Paliokastro (Old Castle), which was built on the site of Classical Pylos at ancient Koryphasion. The castle was built after 1278 by the Frankish (Flemish) ruler of Thebes, Nicholas II de St. Omer, who, after the death of Prince William Villehardouin (1245-1278), married his widow and became regulator of developments in the principate.

Paliokastro was also known as Palaio Navarino or Avarinoi, the root of the last name possibly deriving from the Avars, a barbarian tribe from Central Asia who invaded Western Europe and the Greek peninsula in the 6th c. AD and came as far south as the Peloponnese. The castle is typical of its period and dominates not only the bay of Navarino but also the sea. Paliokastro had a role in all the historical events that were

Fig. 64. Paliokastro and the bay of Voidokilia. Aerial photograph from the south-southwest.

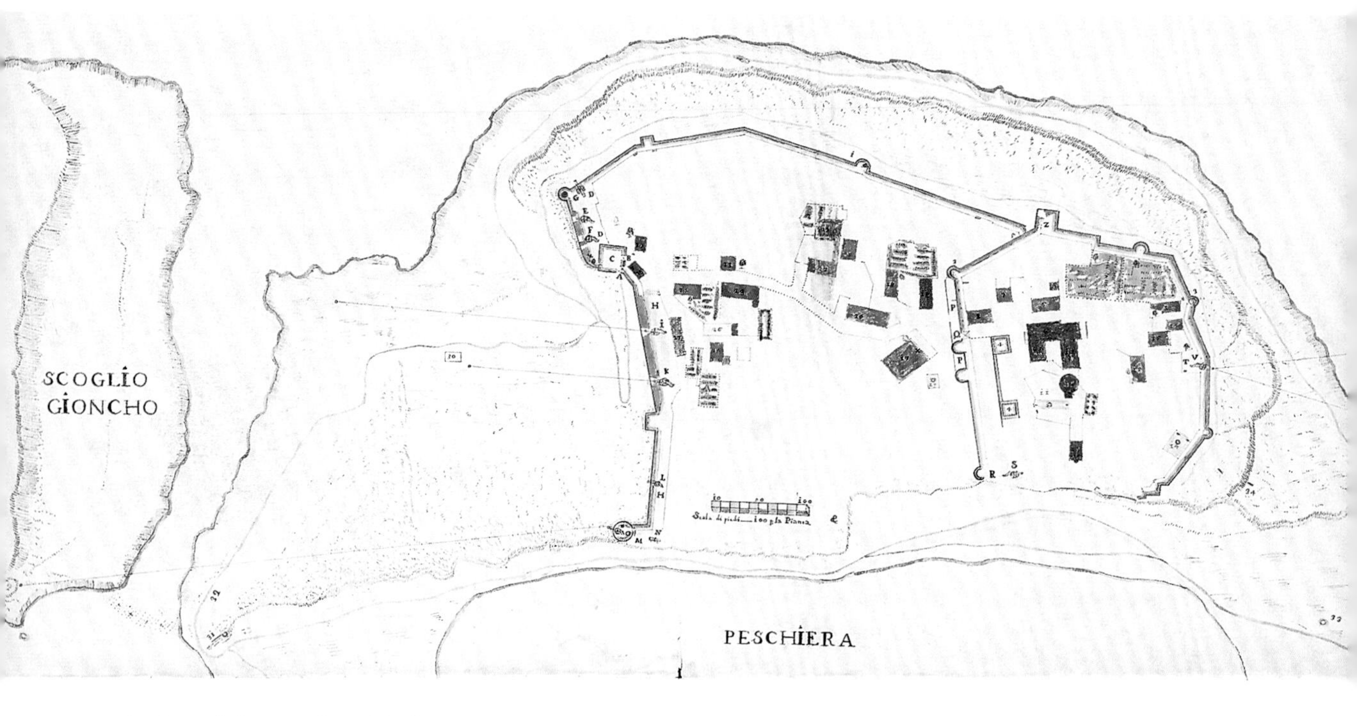

Fig. 65. Paliokastro. Plan of the fortress, drawn by Venetian engineers in 1706.

played out at Pylos. With its tall walls, crenellated battlements, and narrow *chemin de ronde* (communicating corridor), the castle consists of a large enclosure linked with another smaller one at the highest point of Koryphasion. The entrance is in the south wall of the outer enclosure, which has a round bastion at each end. The wall separating the two enclosures has been completely destroyed. There was no natural source of water in the castle and gigantic cisterns were therefore constructed. The enclosure contains several buildings, though these have collapsed, and modern visitors see only a pile of ruins amidst dense vegetation.

The view has been advanced – probably correctly – that the small enclosure lies within the boundaries of the ancient acropolis and the Frankish 13th c. castle. The larger enclosure is the work of the Vene-

Fig. 66. Paliokastro. Views of Koryphasion, drawn by Venetian engineers.

Fig. 67. Paliokastro. View from the south.

tians in the 15th c. and the Turks after 1500. It is highly probable that the latter were responsible for the structure erected to support cannon in the south wall, near the entrance and opposite the Sykia narrows, which is the most vulnerable area of the fortress. Paliokastro is impregnable on the east, where there is a steep cliff, and can be approached only with difficulty from the west, north-west and north. Only the south side, on which a road leads to the entrance, is it easier of access.

For the defenders of Old Navarino, the advantage of height made it possible also to use small cannon placed on the old battlements and fortifications, without the need for special additional building works, and thereby repel the attacks of enemies who may have been better equipped with artillery.

The castle offers an excellent view of the Messenian hinterland and the Ionian sea, where the gaze reaches out to the distant horizon. The sense of vision from Paliokastro is so great that some of the locals maintain that late on a moonless August evening it is possible to see the reflections of the lights of Malta!

Forty years after its construction, Paliokastro was captured by the Genoese, who were attempting to extend the territory they controlled in Greece. Their aim was to use it as a base for attacks on the parts of Messenia occupied by their age-old foes the Venetians.

In 1366, a year of civil strife amongst the Franks, Marie Bourbon, widow of Robert de Taranto, the prince of Achaia, is said to have defended Paliokastro, which was threatened by the united forces of the barons of Achaia, the archbishop of Patra, and her son-in-law, whom she wished to prevent from becoming her successor in the principate.

Fig. 68. Paliokastro. Later building additions, possibly by the Genoese, on the original battlements of the Franks.

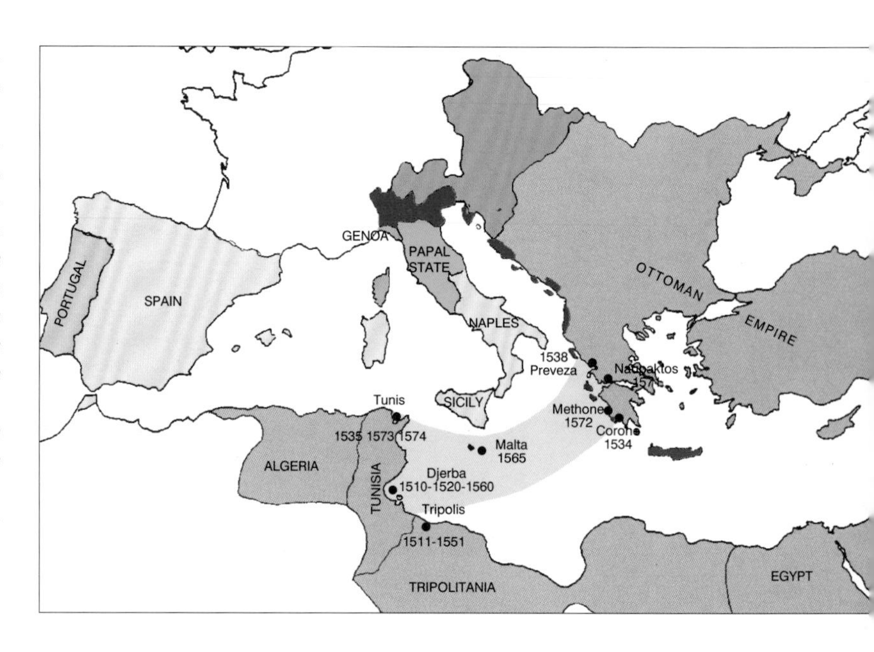

Fig. 69. Map of the Mediterranean showing the clashes between Christian and Ottoman forces during the 16th c.
From the middle of the 15th to the middle of the 16th c. the western Mediterranean was controlled by the Spanish, despite the fact that the Moslems had conquered the north coast of Africa. "The two halves of the Mediterranean were in the sixteenth century two political zones under different banners. Is it therefore surprising that the great sea battles in the time of Ferdinand, Charles V, Sulaiman, and Philip II should repeatedly have taken place at the meeting point of the two seas in the frontier zones" (F. Braudel, The Mediterranean, 1995, p. 136, translated by Sian Reynolds).

In 1381 a military company arrived at Navarino in the form of the Navarre company. This was initially a group of peripatetic mercenary soldiers that gradually acquired such great power that they succeeded the Franks in the Morea. In the final years of life of the principate, Venice bought Paliokastro from its last Frankish ruler, Centurione II Zaccaria of Genoa, in 1423, and entered into an agreement with Mohamed II the Besieger that enabled it to keep the castle for forty years.

In 1437 the emperor of Byzantium Ioannis VIII Palaiologos, the elder brother of Constantine XI, set out from Constantinople by sea, disembarked at Kenchreai, crossed the Peloponnese and came to Navarino. Here he boarded the ship of Patriarch Joseph for a voyage to Rome to engage in his famous discussions with the Pope on the unification of the Churches, which might well have led to a united front against Turkish expansionism (Council of Ferrara-Florence).

The Venetians held Navarino until 1500, when it was taken by the son and successor of Mohamed II, the sultan Bayezid II (1446-1512). The Venetian defender of the castle, Contarini, who fled and surrendered it without a fight to the Turks, was beheaded as a traitor; this was an unjust act, since he was not guilty of cowardice but was simply observing the terms of the Venetian-Turkish treaty. The Venetians recaptured the castle a year later, but the Turks attacked by land and sea and the Venetian defenders were obliged to abandon it once more.

In 1572 Don John of Austria, the commander of the Christian fleet (of Spain, Venice and the forces of Pope Pius V) that had defeated the Turkish armada at Lepanto (Naupaktos) a year earlier, attempted to capture Navarino, but was repelled by the Turks. After he left Navarino, the allied Christian fleet proceeded to Methone and made a surprise attack on some Moslem ships, though without success, while the Turks blocked up the channel of Sykia to make it impossible for ships

Fig. 70. Ioannis VIII Palaiologos. Bronze medallion (1438) with the inscription: ΒΑΣΙΛΕΥΣ ΑΥΤΟΚΡΑΤΩΡ ΡΩΜΑΙΩΝ Ο ΠΑΛΑΙΟΛΟΓΟΣ ΙΩΑΝΝΗΣ (Ioannis Palaiologos, king and emperor of the Romans).

Fig. 71. "The Battle of Naupaktos." Oil-painting on wood.
The Battle of Lepanto (Naupaktos) on 7 October 1571 consolidated Venetian rule in the eastern Mediterranean.

to enter the bay by it. To secure control of the Great Passage at the south, they built a new castle, Niokastro opposite the islet of Sphakteria. Paliokastro was abandoned and thereafter played only an insignificant role in the history of the region.

Fig. 72. Koryphasion with Paliokastro, from the straits of Sykia.

NIOKASTRO

Niokastro, or Neo Navarino, was built at a time when the defensive principles of fortresses dictated by the use of firearms were well established. The expansion of the Ottoman empire into Byzantine territories, as we have seen, coincided with the spread of the use of firearms. The new era of artillery, and at the same time of Turkish domination and power in Europe, might be symbolised by the huge, powerful cannon with which Mohamed II relentlessly pounded the walls of Constantinople in 1453, causing irreparable damage. The first use of firearms had occurred much earlier, however, at the Battle of Crecy during the Hundred Years' War between France and England.

European engineers from the 15th c. onwards studied the new requirements for fortifications imposed by the use of firearms. The new fortresses were based on bastions and were designed to secure protection from the enemy's artillery while exploiting the defender's own artillery to the greatest possible effect. Italian engineers, in particular, developed fortress defence into an art, making mathematical calculations of distances and the form to be taken by the walls, moat and bas-

Fig. 73. Niokastro. Aerial photograph from the south-west.

tions. New concepts of defence were published, and the latest research findings were implemented in fortresses built in Europe and America. Fortified bastions formed the organic element of the new defensive architecture. Fortress walls were no longer erected on steep, rocky, inaccessible heights; they were now no longer thin, tall, and perpendicular, but low, thick, and sloping: low, to reduce as far as possible the target offered to enemy cannon, very thick to withstand artillery bombardment, and sloping inwards to reduce the impact of enemy missiles. Fortresses built by the sea had to be just as strong, to counter enemy warships equipped with cannon.

The Turks kept a close eye on the new techniques of war and employed European engineers, architects, and veterans. They built Niokastro in 1573, two years after the Battle of Lepanto, held it until June 1686, when it was taken by Morosini, and recaptured it when they expelled the Venetians in 1715.

Niokastro is one of the best-preserved fortresses in Greece, and has a history of warfare covering only 257 years. It might be said that the two greatest naval conflicts between Christian Europe and Islam, Lepanto in 1571, the last major naval engagement fought with oared ships, and Navarino in 1827, the last battle with sailing ships, mark out the history of Niokastro: the former obliged the Turks to erect it and the latter compelled them to abandon it forever.

Niokastro is a fortress typical of those created by the new art of defence following the characteristic design. It consists of a large enclosure containing the settlement and linked to a second, smaller enclosure,

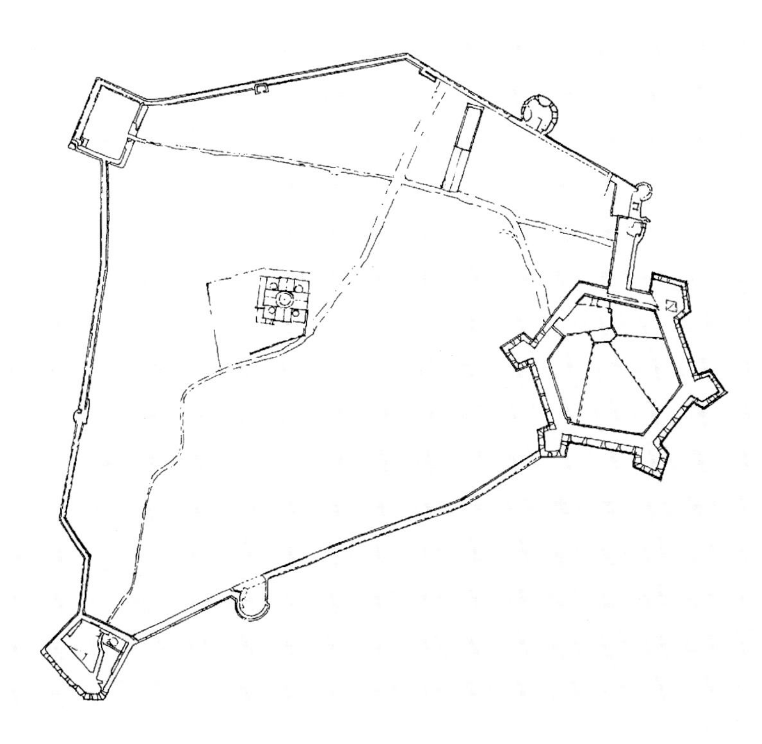

Fig. 74. Niokastro. Plan.

Fig. 75. Niokastro. Depiction of the fortress from the north-east, showing the south end of Sphakteria at the mouth of the bay.

the citadel, which was strongly defended and reinforced by a moat, and a glacis (sloping embankment). The bastions and battlements of the citadel and the large enclosure were made mainly of squared blocks of poros. The gap at the centre of the masonry was filled in with rubble and large bricks and tiles, all set in pozzuolana, a strong mortar compounded of lime, pulverised tiles, and frequently also Theran earth.

On the south and west sides Niokastro is naturally protected by the sea and virtually impassable jagged rocks. The only side from which the castle can be taken is the north or north-east, on which are the road from Pylos to Methone and the nearby slopes of Ai-Nikolas which dominates the bay. The stoutly constructed citadel was designed to withstand enemy attack on this side. Repeated sieges by land and sea, and

Fig. 76. Niokastro. The north-east corner of the fortress with the main, Zematistra gate and the round bastion next to it.

successive captures of Niokastro all left their mark in the form of damage to the walls and bastions. It should be remembered that at the time the fortress was built, portable firearms had a range of 100-150 m. and cannon one of 400-500 m. The first concern of those who made themselves master of the fort was to reconstruct the demolished sections of the walls and block up the gaps as soon as possible, and this is evident in the numerous additions to and reinforcements of the fortifications.

Fig. 77. Niokastro. The main, Zematistra gate of the fortress.

The choice of this particular site for the fortress seems to indicate that the Turks did not attach great importance to the danger of attack from the land, which they believed they controlled, but were mainly concerned to protect the bay by controlling the entrance to it from the sea. This choice and the desire to counter attacks from the sea may be interpreted in the light of their recent naval defeat at Lepanto, and the fact that the Venetian fleet, which ruled the seas, continued to be the main threat to their domination.

The main entrance to Niokastro, the Zematistra, which leads to the fortified settlement in the large enclosure and the entrance to the citadel, is at the north-east corner of the fortress, near the road linking Pylos with Methone. The gate is a tall, imposing structure with a buttress at each corner. The large old wooden two-leaf door, sheathed with iron on both sides, possibly dates from the Second Venetian period. The modern entrance to the fortress from the Pylos side is in the middle of the north wall of the enclosure and consists of an apsidal gateway in which successive building phases can clearly be seen. Two wide paved roads run from the two entrances to the great enclosure and intersect at the building of the Maison Barracks.

At the ends of the west side of the large enclosure wall, overlooking the sea, are two large stout bastions of rectangular plan, that can be entered only from inside the fortress: the so-called Hebdomos at the south-west corner, called *Bateri de marini* or *Forte Santa Barba* by the Venetians, which stands on the rock just above the entrance to the bay,

Fig. 78. Niokastro. The south side of the rectangular north-west bastion (Santa Maria).

Fig. 79. Niokastro. The Hebdomos from the west.

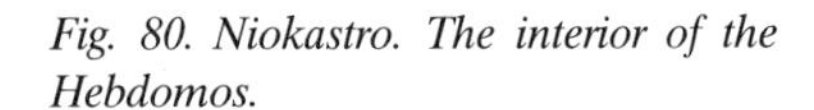

Fig. 80. Niokastro. The interior of the Hebdomos.

and the bastion of Santa Maria at the north-west corner, which controlled the bay just inside the entrance.

The Hebdomos had fifteen cannon placed at two levels. Together with the seven cannon in the nearby circular bastion, now destroyed, and two mounted on the intervening section of the Verga, these created a very strong fortified section of the castle at the south-west entrance to the bay that was defended by twenty-six cannon.

The *chemin de ronde* that ran around three sides of the Hebdomos ended on the west side of the bastion in a wide paved passageway, where there is an array of eight cannon-emplacements facing the sea.

Fig. 81. Niokastro. Isometric drawing of the Hebdomos.

Fig. 82. Niokastro. The west end of the Verga at the Hebdomos. In the distance can be seen the south end of Sphakteria and the rocky islet of Tsichli-Baba.

Fig. 83. Niokastro. Part of the "chemin de ronde" on the west curtain wall of the fortress.

This passageway, which houses the cannon embrasures of the bastion, is supported on four vaults and linked to the floor-level of the courtyard by a sloping paved path, near which is the gunpowder magazine.

It is evident from the great damage and destruction to the three outer sides of the Hebdomos that this was the bastion that sustained most

Fig. 84. Niokastro. The round bastion at the north-east corner of the fortress.

Fig. 85. Niokastro. The small round bastion on the west side of the fortifications, just north of the Hebdomos.

Fig. 86. Niokastro. Interior of the bombed Verga bastion.

Fig. 87. Niokastro. Exterior of the Verga bastion.

of the fire of enemy ships attempting to enter Navarino. The extent of the destruction can be detected in the series of repairs and additions to the masonry and by the replacement of cannon embrasures.

It might be said that this very strong bastion fulfilled the prime aim of the construction of Niokastro, the protection of the entrance to the bay. During the terrible events of 1825, the Hebdomos (the *sea rampart*, as Makriyannis describes it in his *Memoirs*) was blown up by an explosion in the gunpowder magazine. The present, restored form of the bastion is the work of the French under General Maison. The Hebdomos is the start of the south wall of the fortress, which ends at one of the strong bastions of the citadel (bastion III), though it does not communicate with it. The Verga, like the entire enclosure, has a narrow *chemin de ronde* and a large number of loop holes in the parapet between the battlements.

In addition to the Hebdomos and the Santa Maria, there are four more bastions in the large enclosure, which are circular in plan and take the form of a truncated cone. One is near the Zematistra in the north-east corner of the enclosure. A second to the west, known as the Makriyannis bastion, is preserved to its full height near the north entrance, with two interior cannon embrasures. The flat roof of this bastion communicated with ground level by means of a ramp which is no longer preserved. There is a third, small bastion just to the north of the Hebdomos; this had three cannon emplacements without cannon embrasures that communicated with ground level by means of two staircases. The fourth round bastion is in the south side, the Verga. In 1943, during the Italian-German Oc-

Fig. 88. Niokastro. The Verga bastion before it was bombed in 1943, showing the access ramp.

cupation, the fort was bombed by a British aircraft and the Italian munitions blew up, destroying the entire bastion and the paved ramp.

A bastion marked on Venetian drawings in an angle of the fortification wall near the north entrance has left no visible traces and was probably never constructed.

The outer walls of the circular bastions are reinforced by plain buttresses. These bastions have hemispherical roofs built with large tiles, whereas the roofs of the bastions at the citadel moat are vaulted.

Near the centre of the large enclosure in Niokastro stands the church of the Metamorphosis, which was erected as a mosque at the time the castle was built. The Ottoman house of worship was used as a Christian church, however, during the Venetian occupation (1685-1715) and throughout the 1770 uprising (the Orloff episode).

In addition to the basic formal elements of the building, which reveal its original purpose, there is a typical Moslem shrine (mibar) on the east wall inside the building, and the base of the minaret is preserved on the outside at the south-west corner.

Niokastro, like Paliokastro, had no natural source of water, and structures had to be erected to secure a constant supply. Cisterns were built in the large enclosure and the citadel, and two aqueducts were constructed, one starting from Palio Nero near Pylos, on the road to Methone, and the other from the village of Chandrinou, 6 km. from Niokastro. The two met at Kamares, and supplied the fortress with water. A built underground pipe beneath the floor of the great hall in the citadel ended at an open cistern with a fountain at a central point of the large enclosure.

Fig. 89-90. Niokastro. The church of the Metamorphosis, with elevation, section, and groundplan.

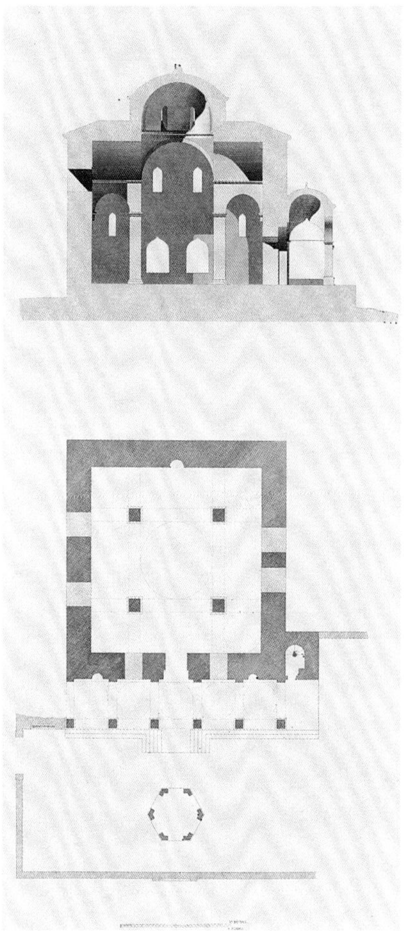

Fig. 91. Niokastro. The church of the Metamorphosis from the south-west.

Fig. 92. Pylos. Part of the Niokastro aqueduct at Kamares, 1 km. from Trion Navarchon Square on the road to Methone.

Fig. 93. Pylos. The high arch spanning the Xeria torrent, carrying a series of smaller arches.

Fig. 94. Pylos. Another part of the Niokastro aqueduct at Ayios Konstantinos, near the Koumbes springs at Chandrinou.

THE CITADEL OF NIOKASTRO

The hexagonal citadel at the highest point of the fortress is entered by a monumental gateway on its west side. The citadel was guarded by five stout bastions, three of which (III, IV, V) were on the moat, which they controlled, and protected the fortress on the east and north-east sides. Bastion II, at the south-west corner of the castle, overlooks the moat and the interior of the large courtyard, while bastion I, at the north-west corner of the citadel, was designed solely to control the interior of the fortress to the west of it. There was probably a sixth bastion, depicted in the Venetian drawings at the north-west angle of the hexagon, but this does not survive. Bastion V has a different plan from the other bastions, and consists of two large rooms, each ending in a cannon embrasure. The exterior walls of the bastions and the fortification walls linking them slope distinctly inwards.

The cannon embrasures are sited in the interior vaulted rooms of the bastions, the *gorgyres*, in such a way that the cannon fired at an oblique angle, thereby securing cross-fire with the neighbouring bastion within the moat.

The walls of the citadel, which are over 8 m. high and 2.50 m. thick, are tough and solid, and are surmounted by battlements with cannon emplacements and long, narrow loop holes.

The passageways of the citadel communicate with the courtyard by way of a ramp on its north side and two interior stone staircases, one on the east and the other on the west side.

The flat roofs of the bastions, which are lozenge-shaped in plan, the wide passageways, 6.50 m. long, and the ramp leading to them, are all paved with cobblestones with a risc of 10-15 cm. In the floor of the flat roofs over the bastions there is an opening measuring 0.40 × 0.60 m.

Fig. 95. Niokastro. Citadel. The ramp leading up to the passageways.

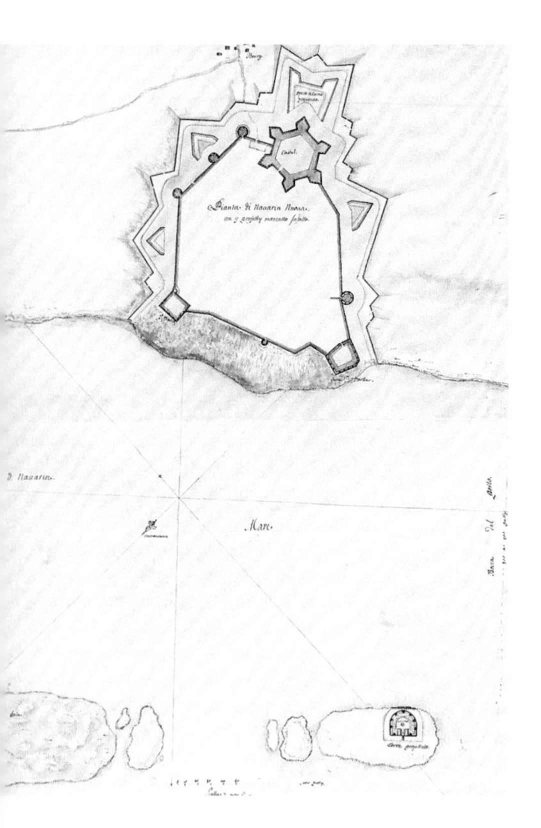

Fig. 96. Niokastro. Drawing of a Venetian proposal to strengthen the castle by extending the outer moat and earthworks.

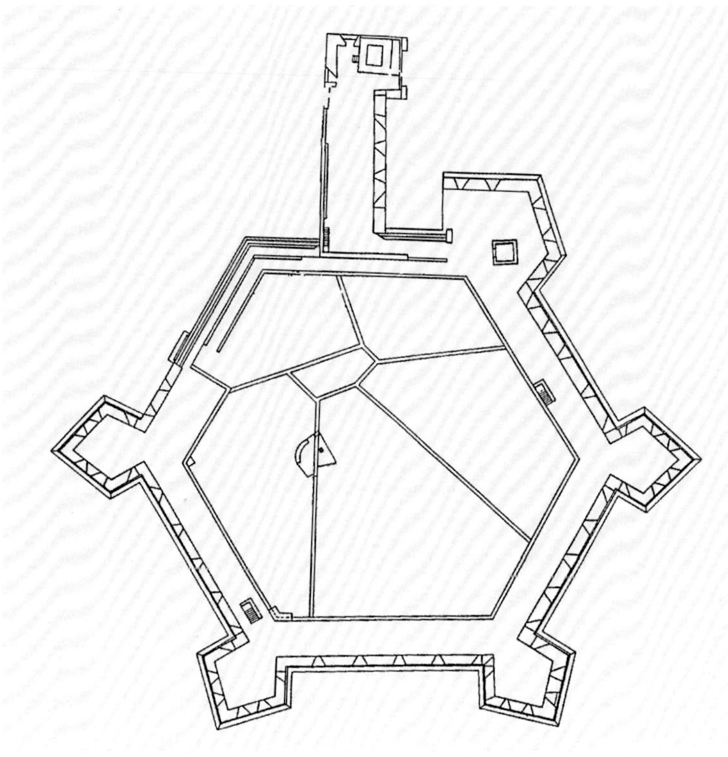

Fig. 97. Niokastro. Citadel. Plan.

Fig. 98. Niokastro. Citadel. Plan under the passageway.

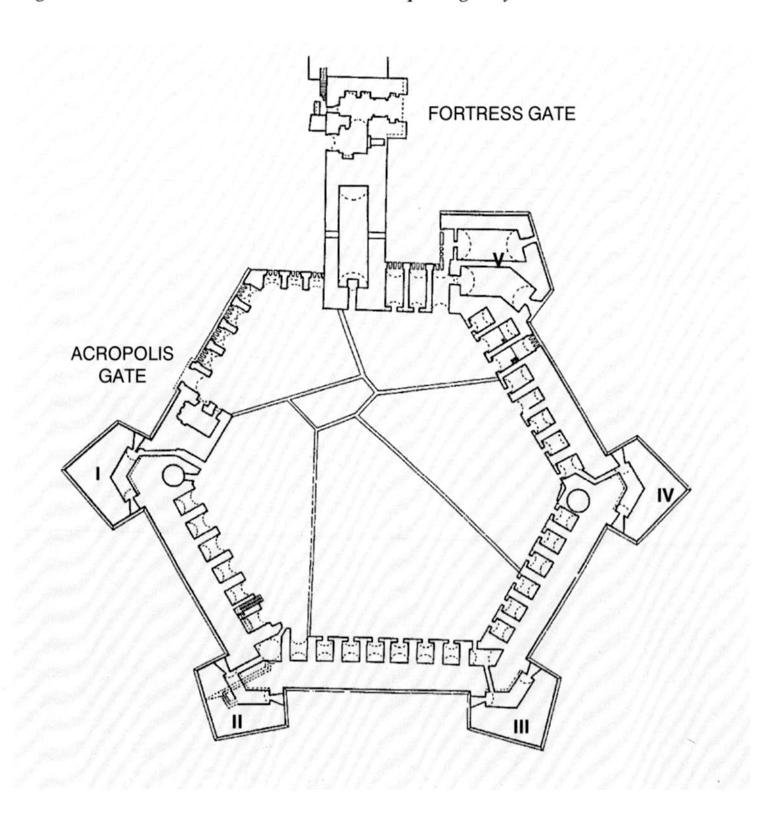

Fig. 99. Niokastro. The east side of the citadel with bastions IV and V.

above each cannon embrasure, to allow the dense, asphyxiating smoke that filled the *gorgyra* after each shot to escape.

The wide, paved passageways made it possible for the defenders to move rapidly and without hindrance, as they carried shells and gunpowder to the cannon during battle.

The citadel was defended by 69 cannon: ten at the cannon embrasures in the *gorgyres* and 59 up on the battlements.

The citadel had its own independent water supply, derived from rainwater. There were three cisterns, one each in bastions I, II and IV, and a larger cistern inside the castle courtyard, to which water was fed by small channels at the side of the passageways, which were given the appropriate slope.

The moat that encloses the main entrance of the fortress and three of the citadel bastions is not a later addition by the Venetians, as has been claimed, but formed part of the original construction. This is clear from the level and position of the cannon embrasures, which form a unified defensive unit designed by the fortress architects of the day to destroy the enemy before the walls. The defence of the citadel was strengthened by the earthworks opposite the walls between bastions III-IV and I-V, which made it difficult for the enemy to approach.

The walls of the citadel and bastions of Niokastro are encircled by an outer cordonne at the level where the vertical parapet of the battlements meets the sloping surface of the wall; this cordonne also determined the height of the passageways.

With Niokastro reinforcing the south-west edge of the Ottoman empire in the Mediterranean, the Turks had a large, secure bay in which they could station their fleet, and a safe base for naval operations that enabled them to bring supplies from Egypt unhindered.

Fig. 100. Niokastro. The gate of the citadel.

Fig. 101. Niokastro. Citadel. Characteristic view of a passageway.

Fig. 102. Niokastro. Citadel. Bastion II. Interior angle of the fortification walls with the battlements, passageways, and arcades.

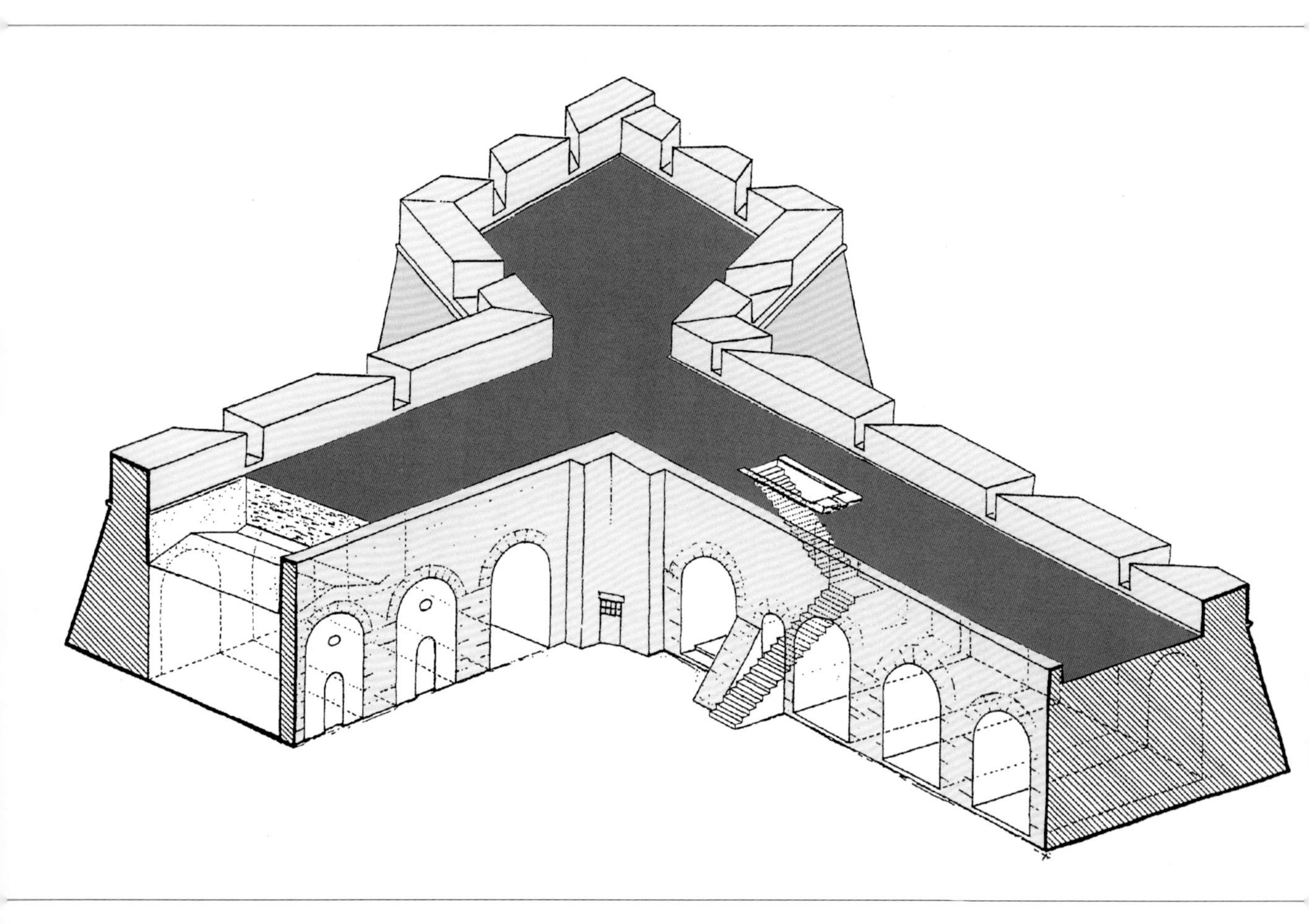

THE ORLOFF EPISODE (1770)

Fig. 103. Catherine II the Great of Russia (1729-1796). Catherine was associated with two liberation movements in Greece, in 1770 (the Orloff episode) and 1792.

In spring 1770, the empress of Russia, Catherine II, who had declared war on the Turks the previous year, sent a squadron of a few ships to Oitylo commanded by two brothers from the Tsar's guard, Alexandros and Theodoros Orloff. The Russians were to incite the Greeks to revolt by persuading them that the time had come for their liberation, with the generous assistance of Russia. This enterprise was to be part of a wider plan for naval and land operations aimed at the destruction of the Ottoman empire.

The years preceding the arrival of the Russians saw a heightening of revolutionary spirit and actions by important figures in the Church, such as the metropolitan bishop of Lakonia, Ananias, whose secular name was Anastasios, the bishop of Methone, Anthimos Karakallos, the bishop of Corone, Makarios Karakallos, and many other liberal clergymen.

The Russians made contact with the notables Panayiotis Benakis from Kalamata and Yiorgos Mavromichalis from the Mani. At Benakis's suggestion, the Greeks and the handful of Russians divided into two legions. One, the eastern legion, consisting of 1,200 Greeks and 20 Russian officers, moved against Mystras, which it captured, putting its Turkish defenders to death; it then went on to Tripoli, but failed to capture the city, and the Greek population was persecuted and slaughtered. The western legion, with 200 Greeks and 12 Russian officers proceeded to Corone by way of Kalamata and Petalidi. Corone was besieged

Fig. 104. The siege of Corone by the Russians under Theodoros Orloff.

but, despite the fact that there had effectively been no maintenance work on the fort since the time the Venetians left, and Turkish morale was low, with the garrison lacking ammunition, the revolted Greeks were unable to take the strong fortress and were obliged to lift the siege after two months. The western legion went on to lay siege to Niokastro by land and sea, with three warships, and the Turks surrendered and handed over their arms after a heavy barrage of cannon fire lasting six days.

The Orloff brothers, believing that the bay of Navarino would form their future base of operations in the Peloponnese, hastily repaired the fortifications of Niokastro, established units on Sphakteria, and began to train Greek rebels. In the atmosphere of optimism generally prevailing after the surrender of Niokastro, grand festivals were organised to raise Greek morale, at which fiery, bombastic proclamations were read out.

Navarino was not secure as long as the fortress and harbour of Methone remained in Turkish hands, and the Orloff brothers therefore laid siege to Methone. Ten days after the start of the siege, however, 8,000 Albanians arrived at Methone and, after fierce fighting, the Greeks and Russians were obliged to raise the siege, abandon their cannon, and seek refuge at Niokastro and Sphakteria. The incredible ferocity of the Albanians, who mercilessly slaughtered, pillaged and burned everything they found in their path, led the Russians to abandon Navarino. Despite the appeals of the Greeks, who tried to delay their departure for a short time to make sure that they themselves could escape, the Russians blew up their munitions, embarked on their ships and left Navarino, taking with them only a few Greek leaders and leaving all the rest without protection, at the mercy of the frenzied Albanians. The lust for slaughter on the part of the latter was of an intensity rarely encountered in the history of Greek tribulations during the period of Turkish domination.

Some idea of it can be derived from the words of an inhabitant of Pylos who took part in the uprising: "*... I ran at once with some of my comrades to save my family. A fearsome sight awaited me. Flames had engulfed our homes. The air was rent by cries of despair. They were the cries of families who were being slaughtered. My own home had been reduced to ashes. I asked the crowds that were fleeing in panic for news of my daughter. I searched amongst the ruins. I came to the cemetery. I saw her clinging to the grave of her mother, struggling despairingly to escape the Albanians who were trying to pull her away. I leapt upon them. I drove them off. I was badly wounded. I fell. And my enemies made off with their victim...*". (K. Simopoulos, *Ξένοι ταξιδιώτες στην Ελλάδα*, II, Athens 1973, p. 680)

After the departure of the Russians the Turks returned to Niokastro and held it for a further 50 years, until the Greek War of Independence (1821-1828). The failed uprising, which is known as the Orloff episode, had tragic consequences: in addition to the many Greeks massacred or enslaved and the reprisals exacted by the Turks, at least 30,000 Greeks left the Peloponnese for the Ionian islands and Sicily. Long after the Orloff episode, the settlements of the Peloponnese, especially those in Messenia, presented a picture of destruction and abandonment.

THE GREEK WAR OF INDEPENDENCE AND THE PHILHELLENES

The early years of the second decade of the 19th century were a period when the entire world echoed to the calls of revolutionary movements. At the beginning of 1820, popular movements demanding constitutional reforms broke out in Spain and Portugal. They were followed by an uprising in the kingdom of Naples that obliged King Ferdinand I to grant a constitution. In South America, Simon Bolivar defeated the Spanish army at Carabobo in 1821, winning independence for Bolivia. Peru proclaimed its independence of Spain and was followed by Guatemala, Mexico, Panama, and Santo Domingo. In Europe, Piedmont rose in revolt in north-west Italy, and an independence movement broke out shortly afterwards in Sicily. All the European revolutionary movements, however, were crushed by the Holy Alliance formed by the reactionary European powers, Austria, Prussia, and Russia.

In a Europe that found itself in turmoil in the aftermath of the industrial revolution and the end of the Napoleonic wars, the Holy Alliance sought to maintain the power of the absolutist regimes by redefining national boundaries. Membership of the Holy Alliance increased to five after the defeat of Napoleon, when it was joined by Great Britain and France. The inspiration behind it was the relentless foe of the Greek uprising, the passionately anti-Greek Metternich, a brilliant diplomat, and minister of Foreign Affairs and later Chancellor of the Habsburg empire.

The Ottoman empire, the "sick man of Europe" became the source of fresh wars, conflicts, diplomatic manoeuvres, and fierce political struggles for spheres of influence.

In 1821, Napoleon the Great died in exile on Saint Helena. Faraday plotted the magnetic field around a conductor carrying an electric current, and the first experiments in thermo-electrical applications were carried out. In England, the railway line to Manchester had been laid a year earlier.

In the European cities in which the fortunes of peoples were decided, neoclassical art and architecture, inspired by ancient Greece, had flourished since the end of the 18th century. It was in this atmosphere that philhellenism developed. This was a period that saw an increased interest in Classical studies, a period during which the views of the romantics had already begun to influence society. For many Europeans philhellenism went far beyond sympathy and support for the subjugated Greeks and was identified with the struggle against barbarity and tyranny in general, a passion for liberty, and a thirst for political and human rights.

The French historian and journalist René Puaux wrote of the exhibition on philhellenism that he organised in Paris in May 1935: *"En Grèce le Philhellénisme n'est pas un phénomène de génération spontané ou provoqué par la Révolution de 1821. Il se rattache à toute la formation de l'esprit français, auquel la Grèce a passé le flambeau durant son éclipse historique."*

Voltaire (1694-1778), one of the leading philhellenes and certainly one of the most fervent supporters of Greek liberation from Turkish domination, wrote that the struggles of this small people against Asia were perhaps the most glorious thing in the world. In July 1770, Voltaire wrote to Catherine II of Russia, who was involved in peace negotiations with the Turks: *"If you make peace* (with the Turks) *what will become of my unfortunate Greeks?"* After the massacre of the Greeks in August, he wrote to

Fig. 105. George Gordon Noel, Lord Byron (1788-1824) wearing Souliot costume.

Fig. 106. François-René Chateaubriand (1768-1848).

Frederick of Prussia: *"This is a mortal blow for me. You know the great celebration I was preparing in the hope that I would see the Greeks of Sophokles and Themistokles free."*

From the beginning to the end of the Greek War of Independence, important intellectuals associated themselves and their activities, and indeed their very work, with the Greek revolutionary impulse. Delacroix (1798-1863), the greatest of the French romantic painters, expressed his horror and revulsion at the massacre at Chios in his painting of this name, a harbinger of his painting entitled "Greece expiring at Messolongi". Chateaubriand (1768-1848) created an active philhellene movement in Paris. In 1824, the French historian and philologist Fauriel (1772-1844) published his *Folk Songs of Modern Greece* in two volumes.

Powerful Greek voices were heard with increasing clarity by the giants of the European intellectual world.

The Russian poet Alexander Sergeyevich Pushkin (1799-1837) wrote:

Forward, stand straight revolted Greece
hold firm your weapons,
not in vain has Olympos risen up,
Pindos and Thermopylai – your glory.

From the depth of your bowels
liberty has sprung forth, bright, courageous
from the tomb of Sophokles, from the marbles
of Athens, still sacred and young.

Home of gods and heroes, you are suddenly
breaking your yoke and adverse fortune,
to the sound produced by the worthy lyre
of your own Tyrtaios, of Byron and of Rhigas.

(D. Photiadis, *Η επανάσταση του Εικοσιένα*, I, Athens 1971-72, p. 386)

Goethe (1749-1832), transported by the flame and passion for liberty of Greece in revolt, felt, in the person of Euphorion – Byron in *Faust* – intense exaltation: *"To ascend ever higher! To look ever further!"*

Shelley (1792-1822) wrote a tragedy called Greece on analogy with the *Persians* of Aeschylus, prophesying the victory of the Greeks over the Turks.

On the occasion of Lord Byron's death at Messolongi, Lamartine wrote:

One final cry was left to you, and you uttered it,
Your tongue had only a single word...
Freedom.

(Photiadis, op.cit., p. 180)

Lord Byron (1788-1824) was already a famous poet when he came to Greece in January 1824 to take part in the Greek Uprising.

THE BEGINNING OF THE NATIONAL LIBERATION STRUGGLE (1821)

In February 1821, Alexandros Ypsilandis, a Greek Phanariot and general in the Russian army, assumed the leadership of the Greek secret revolutionary organisation known as the *Philiki Etairia* ("Friendly Society"). At the head of a small, picked band of Greeks, Ypsilandis crossed the river Prouthos, at the time the boundary between Russia and Romania, which was held by the Ottoman Turks, resigned from the Tsar's army, and declared the beginning of the Greek Uprising at Jassy.

The Greek nobleman, who had lost his right arm in 1812 fighting Napoleon's French as an officer of the Tsar, initiated the uprising at a time when the Holy Alliance was meeting at Laibach (Ljubljana) to discuss how to deal with and defeat the revolutionary movements in Europe. The participants in this conference, which was presided over by Metternich, were Austria, Russia, Prussia, France, and England.

Ypsilandis, a Russian general and defender of the Russian empire, who had instigated the Greek Uprising from Russian soil, wrote a letter requesting Russia's backing for the struggle for Greek liberation. Thanks to Metternich's intervention, however, the Russian emperor rejected Ypsilandis's request; ironically, the imperial reply was drafted by the Russian Foreign Minister, Count Ioannis Kapodistrias, who was destined to become the first prime-minister of Greece in 1828. After the defeat at Dragatsani (7 June 1821), Alexandros Ypsilandis was arrested in Transylvania by the Austrians. This ardently revolutionary figure was released from jail in 1827; two months later Ypsilandis died in Vienna at the age of 36, worn out by the hardship of his six years of imprisonment. Although it failed, Ypsilandis's rebellion supplied the spark for the general Greek uprising.

From one end of the national territories to the other, Greeks arose against the Turks. By March 1822, there had been outbreaks of rebellion ranging from Crete to Macedonia.

At this time, the population of the Peloponnese, Central Greece and Euboea consisted of 705,850 Greeks and 63,600 Turks.

In the Peloponnese, the Greeks made themselves masters of the fortresses or shut the Turks up in them. This was also the case with the forts of Messenia. The bishop of Methone, Grigorios Papatheodorou, himself a member of the Philiki Etairia, together with the local chieftains, managed to confine the Turks to the fort of Methone on 29 March 1821. Leaving a garrison of 300 men there, he then moved on to Pylos to take part in the uprising organised by the Ikonomidis brothers of Pylos, also members of the Philiki Etairia. The Greeks laid siege to Niokastro in April 1821 and captured it on 7 August af-

Fig. 107. Prince Alexandros Ypsilandis (1792-1828) crossing the Prouthos.

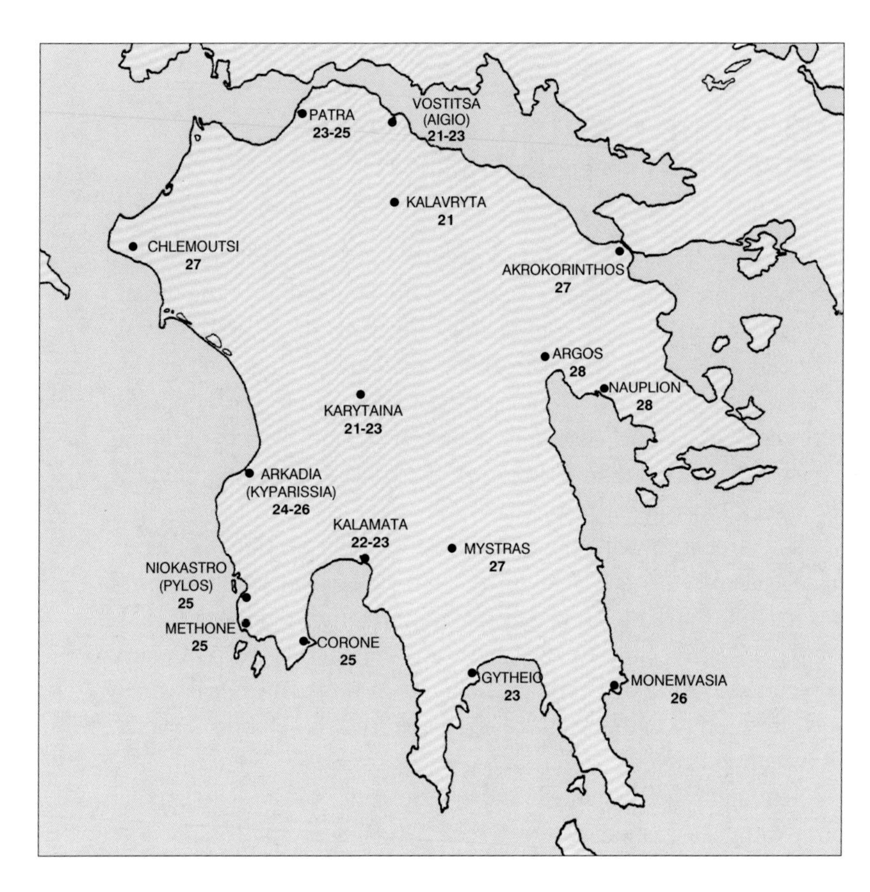

Fig. 108. Map of the Peloponnese showing the dates of the first clashes of the Greek War of Independence and the besieging of the Turks in the castles, in March 1821.

ter a siege lasting several months. The Turks soldiers and inhabitants of Niokastro taken prisoner are said to have been abandoned on the islet of Chelonisi in the bay, where they died of hunger and thirst.

Paliokastro fell to the rebels directly afterwards, but down to the end of the War of Independence, the Greeks never succeeded in capturing the forts of Methone and Corone.

Fig. 109. Andreas Miaoulis (1769-1835), leader of the Greek fleet during the War of Independence.

"POISONOUS DAY" (1825)

– George, why are you dressing yourself and donning your weapons?
– I'm going to go to Niokastro, where the war is,
and if there's fighting and I'm slain, and if they kill me without cause,
I have no mother to weep for me, no lady to mourn me.
– Your youth will weep for you, your weapons will mourn you.
(G. Tarsouli, *Μωραΐτικα τραγούδια,* Athens 1944)

Fig. 110. Mohamed Ali, the pasha of Egypt (1769-1849) and father of Ibrahim pasha.
As recompense for his collaboration in the attempt to suppress the Greek uprising, through the campaign of his son Ibrahim in the Peloponnese (1824-1827), the Turks granted him Crete, which he held until 1841, and Thasos, which remained under Egyptian rule until 1908.

The Greeks held Niokastro, Paliokastro and the surrounding area until 1825. This was a difficult year. Because of political conflicts, the experienced leaders had been replaced or were in jail, and those in charge of the military operations were unfit to direct the liberation struggle. It was against this background that Ibrahim Pasha of Egypt, son of Mohamed Ali, disembarked at Methone in February with his first military units and began his lightning campaign in the Peloponnese. The revolutionary government at Nauplion failed to take action, and Ibrahim therefore had ample time to disembark increasing numbers of troops from Egypt at Methone.

Ibrahim realised at once that neither Methone nor Corone, where he moved quickly to disperse the Greek besiegers, could serve as a base for his fleet. The bay of Navarino was ideal for this purpose, and in order to facilitate his advance through the entire Peloponnese, he made his first aim the capture of the two fortresses protecting the bay and the establishment of good communications between Niokastro and Methone. The revolutionary government acted only after a criminal delay, sending ships and an army to the area to reinforce the forts. The bay of Navarino quickly became the centre of revolutionary operations. Even before his first reinforcements arrived, Ibrahim bombarded Niokastro remorselessly, in a harbinger of the major operation he later organised to capture Sphakteria and Navarino. On 15 March, the Egyptians attacked Schinolakka, but were repulsed with great losses, and on 7 April,

Fig. 111. Ibrahim pasha (1789-1848). Ibrahim was born in Kavala, and his name is linked with some of the most horrific incidents in Greece under Turkish domination.

Fig. 112. Panayiotis Zographos, "SIEGE AND BATTLES OF NAVARINO 1825".

Explanatory legend for the painting.
– 1. Neokastron, which Ibrahim besieged with all his forces. – 2. Ibrahim's tents. – 3. Ibrahim's army that fought against Neokastron with cannon, balls, and rifles. – 4. Arkadia, Philiatra, and Gargalianoi, which were held by Makriyannis. – 5. When Makriyannis was at Gargalianoi, Katzis Mavromichalis (who was in the Castle) went to him and said: "Those who are under siege chose me to go to Chores and I went, where Kountouriotis was with all the chieftains, about 15,000 men, for him to send and capture Old Navarino, so that the enemy wouldn't capture it and put us in danger. I told him, no one would capture it, and I came to you, Markiyanni, and I tell you, and what you tell me, I'll tell the besieged. I'll take my corps and go and capture them; and I'll move at once." – 6. Makriyannis with his corps and a very few Arkadians (under Anag. Papatzoris), no more than three hundred and fifty men in all, holds the position of Navarino. – 7. Papatzoris and the Arkadians occupy the strait. – 8. The next day, very early, the Turks came, both infantry and cavalry, and passed over the bridge of Vivari, and battle was joined and lasted for five hours; and the Greeks retreated from the bridge fighting with great courage, and afterwards they departed. A very few Turks were killed, and three Greeks were wounded. They came out again the following day, and had no appetite for battle; and there were only skirmishes. – 9. After a few days those who were shut up inside invited Makriyannis to go in, and he went with 116 men, and left the rest in the same position (it was Easter Sat-

urday). – 10. On Easter Monday Ibrahim set out to go and destroy the few men left behind by Makriyannis at Navarino. Then, the besieged, Velentzas, Stephos and many others, and Makriyannis himself, were compelled to come out and face the enemy on the cannon emplacements and killed several of them; and Ibrahim was compelled to turn back. Eleven Greeks were killed or wounded. – 11. Ibrahim sent a messenger demanding that the Greeks surrender, and when they refused he embarked his forces on the ships and fought, and made a landing on Sphakteria and destroyed the Greeks; about 900 Greeks were drowned or killed, and then he took Old Navarino. – 12. Sphakteria with the Greek dead and drowned. – 13. Tzamados, Anagnostaras, Simos, Sainis and many other leaders were destroyed there. – 14. Tsamados's ship, with Mavrokordatos and Saktouris fights its way out. – 15. Greek ships. – 16. The frigates force their way in and attack the castle. When the basic essentials for the castle, above all the water, had been saved, they sent Makriyannis and made a treaty with Ibrahim, and embarked. – 17. Chores and Kountouriotis with the Greeks sat there. The besieged G. Mavromichalis, Io. Mavromichalis (who was killed), P. Yiatrakos, D. Saktouris, N. Lambros Kranidiotis, the Kallergides, Gardikiotis, G. Livaditis, G. Velentzas, Stephos, various Greeks, Phocians and other brothers that I don't remember, and Makriyannis.

Fig. 113. General Ioannis Makriyannis (1797-1864), who served as Military Governor of Athens and commander of the Acropolis garrison. After the creation of the Greek state, he played a leading role in the events of 3 September 1843 to secure a Constitution for Greece.

3,250 Greeks were defeated in a bloody encounter at Kremmydi, leaving 600 dead on the battlefield.

Makriyannis, one of the most important Greek leaders of the War of Independence, brought a force of Roumeliots from Gargalianoi to the abandoned, unprotected Paliokastro – Avarinoi, as he calls it – where he organised resistance against Ibrahim's Egyptians before moving on to Niokastro. Turkish-Egyptian crews disembarked on Sphakteria and, after a fierce hand-to-hand struggle, succeeded in decimating the Greeks defending the islet. This was one of the greatest massacres during the entire War of Independence.

Makriyannis describes the massacre in his *Memoirs* as follows: *"... and they gave us no peace night and day: battle without end. The fort was rotten and falling to bits: we patched it up with wooden caissons which we filled with earth. We worked and fought day and night and were exhausted. Most of us were sick by reason of our unceasing labour and thirst. Ibrahim's gunners and engineers were all Frenchmen, and they laid the fort in ruins."*

The Greek dead numbered 350, with Anagnostaras, Yiannis Mavromichalis, Tsamados, and Sachinis amongst them. The Italian Count Santa Rosa was also killed at this time.

The eight Greek ships that had been left at Navarino by Admiral Miaoulis of Hydra to supply the besieged in Niokastro managed to break through the ring of Egyptian ships and escape.

The *Ares*, the ship owned by the sea-warrior Tsamados from Hydra, which had taken part in most of the naval engagements during the War of Independence, found itself left behind and alone at the exit from the bay. It was captained not by Tsamados, who had been killed in the fighting on Sphakteria, but by Nikolaos Votsis, who was actually the captain of another ship that had managed to leave the bay shortly before under the command of a different captain. The *Ares* itself escaped after a titanic struggle.

Makriyannis writes of these dramatic events: *"... Sachtouris, the garrison commander of Niokastro got aboard Tsamados's ship, and escaped amid great danger, after a battle with all the Turkish ships, through the indescribable bravery shown by the crew of the ship. It was one thing to see this and another to tell of it. They escaped by the grace of God, who gave them such great courage."*

The same events are described in greater detail by Spyridon Trikoupis: *"And the Greek ships, having taken on their sailors, cut their anchors and sailed out unharmed, until the mouth of the harbour was tightly closed; the 'Ares' hung back, hoping that Tsamados would be saved, and meantime the enemy ships closed the mouth of the harbour by moving close together ... And just as the sailors cut the anchors and spread their sails to sail out through the enemy fleet ... the 'Ares' advanced as far as the mouth of the harbour, that mouth of Hell, under cannon fire from ahead, astern, right and left; the 'Ares' itself returned the cannon fire constantly, defended itself, advanced, and after great suffering, escaped the threat posed by these ships, but soon fell amongst many more. For three hours it*

Fig. 114. The brig "Ares" was commissioned by Anastasios Tsamados, a wealthy merchant from Hydra, and built in Venice in 1807.
On 16 March 1825, Tsamados and the "Ares" brought food and munitions to Niokastro, which was besieged by Ibrahim. After the achievement of Greek independence the "Ares" was purchased by the Greek state and used for training purposes.

struggled amidst swarms of ships, and this terrible struggle removed its spanker, holed its sails, crushed its helm and cut its yards; and as the sailors moved about the deck, they trod on the spent cannonballs which constantly fell like rocks from the enemy ships and lay strewn about the entire deck of the 'Ares'."

(Spyridon Trikoupis, *Ιστορία της Ελληνικής Επαναστάσεως*, II, Athens 1879, p. 208-209)

The bay of Navarino was full of bodies. The defenders of Niokastro, unable to assist, looked on in anguish at the massacre of their compatriots and the capture of Sphakteria by the Egyptians.

Of this tragic day, Makriyannis, who was in Niokastro, wrote in his *Memoirs*:

"That day, brother readers was poison for the country, which lost so many gallant lads and men of position, both soldiers and sailors. For all the country that day was poison, and for us it was like death itself, for we lost our comrades. The battle now grew fiercer. Our position was extended and we were few. Not a drop of water. Sleepless day and night. And the leading commanders of our country were looking on from the high ground without stirring a finger. Such vast forces were gazing at us through their glasses as if we were not their brothers and comrades in arms. They saw us, and they could hear the death song from the mouths of those very cannon of ours which were cutting us to pieces. The lagoon was full of drowned men like frogs in a march; just so they floated in the water. And the island was full of corpses. And the Greek forces looked at us from afar off."

Ibrahim's success on Sphakteria marked the beginning of defeat for the Greeks. The defenders of Paliokastro capitulated on 30 April 1825. Bishop Grigorios was captured and imprisoned in the Bourtzi,

COUNT SANTORE SANTA ROSA

Fig. 115. Santore Santa Rosa. Minister of Military Affairs in the Piedmont government, which was overthrown by the Austrians (April 1821). The Italian revolutionary and nobleman (born 1773) was a philhellene. He came to Greece after the uprising in December 1824 and was killed on Sphakteria in April 1825.

"I love Greece with a love that has something exceptional in it. The Greek people, good and noble, who have lived for centuries as slaves, are our own brothers. Italy and Greece share common fortunes, and since I can do nothing for my fatherland, I am obliged to devote to Greece the few years and little strength remaining to me." So writes the great Italian philhellene.

From Tripoli, Santa Rosa wrote a letter to the commander of the Egyptian artillery, the Italian colonel Romaiu, his colleague in the revolutionary government of Piedmont and his deadly foe in Greece. The ardent revolutionary, unaware that Romaiu, in the enemy camp, was corresponding with the revolutionary committee in Zakynthos and supplying the Greeks with valuable information about the Egyptian movements and plans, wrote: *"Our ancestors fought in Crete, were victorious at Lepanto, and bathed the mountains of Attiki and the Peloponnese in their blood to prevent the Turks gaining a footing in Europe. Shall we, the descendants of these brave men, dishonour the name of Italy on the same territory? Come and join the brave, whom honour, not love of violence, impels towards danger..."*

To the pro-Turkish French colonel Slue, who changed his name to Suleiman bey and served in Ibrahim's army, Santa Rosa wrote: *"...You are a coward and a craven. You are a man without honour. I challenge you to a duel. If you dare, come; I'm waiting for you..."*

Santa Rosa, who was besieged by Ibrahim's Egyptians in Niokastro, said as he embarked on the *Ares* to go to Sphakteria: *"I shall go to Sphakteria. I cannot watch from the battlements of Niokastro a contest that I love so much and that my heart desires."*

Before disembarking on the island, he said to those who were urging him to remain on board the ship: *"... No. It's impossible for me to stay. I want to see the Turks at close quarters with my rifle..."*

Santa Rosa was killed on Sphakteria and is honoured as a hero. Before he died, he commented prophetically: *"We shall die, but the Peoples will conquer."*

the tower at Methone, where he died after being horribly tortured. On 11 May, Niokastro also surrendered.

Like a gigantic bastion, the three fortresses of Methone, Corone and Niokastro offered a very strong base from which Ibrahim could launch his raids on the Peloponnese, and also from which he could communicate with Egypt to procure supplies and reinforcements. In December 1825, Ibrahim's fleet sailed from the bay of Navarino to deliver the *coup de grâce* to Messolongi.

The Turkish-Egyptians held the fortresses of Messenia and all the other areas they captured in 1825 for two and a half years.

In the autumn of 1826, the French interpreter at Constantinople, Charles Deval, who visited Methone, provided a characteristic picture of the situation there at this period: *"But the most moving spectacle, the most grievous, was the slave market at Methone ... The slaves were mostly women of all ages. There were also a few children, all of them under 16 years, because those older than this had been put to death or shut up in prisons. They had been taken prisoner at Messolongi by the repulsive Arabs, partly for their debauchery, though more for profit ... I also saw other fearful things. Twenty heads, recently severed, were thrown up by the waves at my feet. I inquired of a passerby and he told me indifferently that a few prisoners had been executed in the prison. Shortly afterwards I saw about a hundred prisoners approaching accompanied by black guards. The faces of these unfortunates were bright yellow. Marks made by the lash could be seen on their backs and arms. They were carrying enormous beams on their shoulders. When they passed in front of the heads that were rolling in the sand, they turned their gaze, noticed them, riveted their eyes on them, shuddered, and changed colour. Perhaps they would suffer the same fate. Most of these prisoners were shepherds. They were taken as they grazed their flocks and put in chains by the Arabs ... In the tower* [Bourtzi], *the prisoners were lying not on straw mattresses but in the mud created by the seawater that came in through the cracks in the walls. A filthy, dark place. I could barely make out their features by the light of a lamp, piled up on each other as they were ... With my own eyes I saw fifty farmers taken before Ibrahim's pavilion, branded with burning iron, and thrown into a filthy prison, where they had to lie in a heap in the mud, waiting for a ship to take them to Egypt, a place far from the soil of their beloved homeland, which they would water with their sweat and tears as they laboured for Mehmet Ali. I saw priests crucified, tied to olive-trees, being burned with a slow fire, I saw ... but enough."*

(K. Simopoulos, *Πώς είδαν οι ξένοι την Ελλάδα του '21*, 5 (1826-1829), Athens 1984, p. 99-109)

Fig. 116. The British admiral Sir Edward Codrington (1770-1851).

THE BATTLE OF NAVARINO (1827). CAUSES, CONTRADICTIONS AND OUTCOME OF THE CONFLICT

On 20 October 1827, the bay of Navarino was the stage for the final act of the Greek War of Independence, the naval engagement that brought the allied fleet of Britain, France and Russia into conflict with the Turkish-Egyptian fleet.

The three European powers had agreed by the Treaty of London (6 July 1827) to create a semi-autonomous Greek state paying tribute to the Sultan. Although many of the chieftains were disappointed with the agreements entered into by the three powers, the treaty was accepted by the revolutionary government. To Greece's good fortune, however, it was categorically rejected by the sultan, who considered that the Europeans were trying to dictate terms to him in his own empire.

The year 1827 was a very unfortunate, difficult year for the Greek Uprising: Tripolis had long since fallen into the hands of the Turks. The fall of Messolongi was followed by that of the fortress of Athens, the Acropolis. The Turks had taken all the castles in the Peloponnese with the exception of Nauplion and Monemvasia; in these two regions and the Mani, the flame of the uprising still burned bright. The Greeks were still engaged in their fratricidal conflicts: Karaiskakis, Athanasios Diakos, Papaphlessas, Botsaris, and Odysseas Androutsos had all been lost, and Ibrahim was pillaging, killing and burning, sowing death and destruction. Everyone knew that his next target was Hydra, the leading Greek naval power in the Aegean, the great heart of the Uprising.

The Turkish-Egyptian fleet of 89 ships, under the command of the Turk Tachir pasha and the Egyptian admirals Mustafa bey and Ibrahim's brother-in-law Mocharem bey, entered the bay of Navarino to reinforce and supply Ibrahim's land forces that were devastating the Peloponnese.

The European fleet consisted of the British contingent of twelve warships and the flagship *Asia*, under Vice-admiral Codrington, the Russian, of eight ships and the flagship *Azov*, under Vice-admiral Heyden, and the French, of seven ships and the flagship *Siren*, under Vice-admiral Derigny. This fleet entered the bay in accordance with a secret article of the Treaty of London agreed in July, which approved of the use of "whatever measures the situation requires" in the interests of achieving peace and compelling Ibrahim to desist from his killing and looting.

The naval encounter began with a "trivial" event: light boats were used during the negotiations between the rival leaders, plying between the flagships, and Petros Mikelis, the pilot of the *Asia*, who was acting as interpreter, was shot and killed. Mikelis was accompanying a British officer who was proceeding by light boat to the Egyptian flagship *Warrior* for the negotiations.

The battle, the last major naval engagement fought by sailing ships, lasted four hours and resulted in the sinking of 60 Turkish-Egyptian ships, with the loss of 6,000 sailors. During the conflict the Turkish-Egyptians fired cannon rounds from the bastions of Niokastro that overlooked the sea and from Sphakteria, the south end of which they had fortified. The allied fleet lost not a single ship, but 272 British sailors were killed, along with 198 Russians and 185 French. It may be noted that all three allied flagships had Greek pilots, and that there were French officers serving with the Egyptian fleet; one of these, Letellier, prepared and organised the disposal of the Turkish-Egyptian fleet in the bay of Navarino. Just before the battle began, Letellier was informed by the French in the allied fleet that he should disembark from his ship.

The three admirals and many of the other officers and men have left moving descriptions of the battle in their memoirs and writings.

The following is from the account by a British sailor aboard the *Genoa*:

"The face of the water was covered with pieces of wreck; masts and yards drifted about on the surface, to which clung hundreds of poor wretches whose vessels had been blown up. Numbers of them imploringly cried upon us, in the Turkish language, a small smattering of which most of us had picked up at Smyrna."

(C.M. Woodhouse, *The Battle of Navarino*, 1965, p. 132)

The same sailor tells us (op. cit., p. 125):

"After this it was, Fire away, my boys, as hard as you can! The first man that I saw killed in our vessel was a marine, and it was not till we had received five or six rounds from the enemy. He was close beside me. I had taken the sponge out of his hand, and on turning round saw him at my feet with his head fairly severed from his body, as if it had been done with a knife. The firing continued incessant, accompanied occasionally by loud cheers, which were not drowned even in the roar of the artillery, but distincter than these could be heard the dismal shrieks of the sufferers, that sounded like death knells in the ear, or like the cry of war-fiends over their carnage.

About half an hour after the action had commenced, two boys of the names of Fisher and Anderson, the one about 14 years of age, the other about 12, both servants to the officers in the wardroom, were standing on the after-hatchway gratings, nearly abreast of the gun I was quartered at, on the lower deck. They were both fine looking boys, and neatly dressed in jacket and trowsers. Fisher, indeed, was the most interesting boy I ever saw. His cheeks were blooming with health, and his large black eyes were shaded by long black curled hair. They were standing, as I said, on the gratings, hand-in-hand, and raising their tiny voices amidst the cheers of our men. I was loading the gun, and not a moment before, had cried to Fisher to go to the fore magazine for some tubes, when a shrill shriek sounded in my ears, and turning round, I saw Fisher lying a lifeless corpse. Anderson had also fell wounded, but not mortally.

He crawled across to the corpse of Fisher, and burying his head in

Fig. 117. The Russian admiral Count Longinos Heyden (1772-1840).
Heyden was leader of the Russian Mediterranean fleet in Greece, and after the battle of Navarino contributed to the task of the prime minister, Ioannis Kapodistrias.

Fig. 118. The French admiral Henri Daniel Gauthier Derigny (1782-1835).
In 1822, Derigny received the rank of captain and was placed in charge of the French naval squadron in the Aegean.

Fig. 119. Panayiotis Zographos, "The Battle of Navarino" (1834).

THE BATTLE OF OLD NAVARINO
Explanatory legend for the painting.
– 1. The fort of Neokastron. – 2. The island of Sphakteria, which was held by the Turks who had on it their tents, cannon, and camp, as also on the nearby islet and Old Navarino, and they fought when the ships of the three Powers entered the bay, 27 in all. – 3. The Turkish warships and burned ships. – 4. The Turkish cargo ships. – 5. The feluccas leaving with the Turks and capturing the mountains on the land, and the drowning. – 6. The island in the harbour. – 7. Divari and its bridge. – 8. The fire-ship that burned. – 9. And four more.

his dead companion's bosom, uttered the most piercing cries I ever heard. Another and I were ordered to take him to the cockpit. We found Fisher had been struck by a shot on the back of the head. A smile was still on his lips, and his cheeks were as ruddy as ever. It was with great difficulty we could separate little Anderson from the body of his comrade. He implored us not to take his 'dear Ned' from him. Surrounded as we were with death and danger, it was impossible not to be affected at this scene; but we were obliged to use force and tear him away. The poor boy's sufferings were not complete; for as he was being taken to the cockpit, a splinter struck his right arm and broke it. Fisher was laid down among the common heap of slain, to await a watery grave.

The battle at this time was raging with the most relentless fury; vessel after vessel was catching fire; and when they blew up they shook our ship to its very kelson. We sustained a most galling fire from the two-line-of-battle ships abreast of us, which kept playing upon us till they were totally disabled by having all their masts shot away, and whole planks tore out of their sides, by the enormous discharge of metal from our guns.

Cool, however, as a British sailor is in danger, nothing can approach the Turk in this respect. Some of the crew of the French frigate 'Alcyone' had picked up a Turk, who by his dress appeared to be a person of rank in their navy. When he was brought aboard, he found his arm so shattered that it would need to undergo an amputation; so he made his way down the cock-

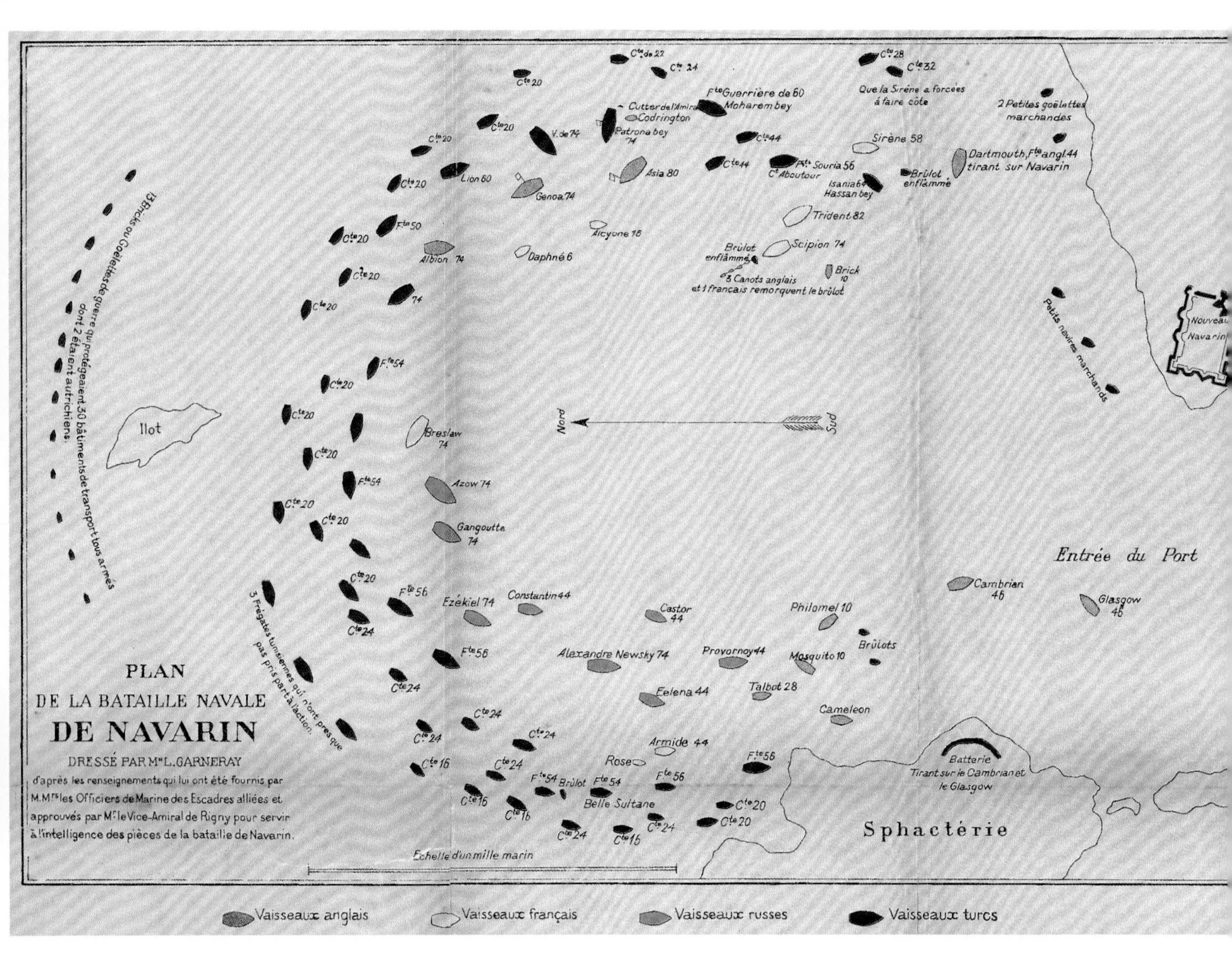

Fig. 120. The battle of Navarino. The dispositions of the fleets in the bay of Navarino.

pit ladder with as much ease as if he had not been hurt, and as much dignity as if he had made a prize of the frigate. He pointed to his shattered arm, and made signs to the surgeon that he wanted it off. The surgeon obliged him so far, and having bound up the stump and bandaged it properly, the Turk made his way to the deck, and plunging into the water, swam to his own vessel, that was opposed along with another to the very frigate he had been aboard of. He was seen climbing the side with his one arm, but had not been aboard many minutes, when it blew up, and he, among others of the crew, in all probability perished in the explosion."

Captain Milius of the *Scipion* gives the following description of his experience, relating to a fire-ship that took part in the battle: (Woodhouse, op. cit., p. 117):

"This devilish device, under the direction of men who were as skilful as they were brave, succeeded in attaching itself to the port side of my ship and gradually slid under the bowsprit, and tangled with the spritsail and the cathead. We tried vainly to drive it back into open water. It really seemed as if it were drawn to us by a magnetic force. The jib, the bowsprit, and the ropes of the foreward masts became a prey to the flames which were driven aft by a fairly strong breeze, blowing from the

south, so that they spread into the 36-gun battery by the hawse-holes and the port-holes. A number of top-men plunged into the fire to put it out; some of the gunners were scorched at their posts; others were seriously wounded by the explosion of powder-kegs bursting into flames in their arms. The flames gained a hold three times in different parts of the ship, but the remarkable thing is that throughout the fire our brave gunners never once ceased to fire on the Turkish ships and the fort which had its guns trained at maximum depression on the 'Scipion'. Never was a ship in a more critical situation. While the brave seamen plunged into the blazing furnace under the bowsprit to halt the progress of the flames, I let out the anchor-chain which held the ship, and set the main-sail and the fore-topsail so as to turn before the wind, intending by this desperate manoeuvre, at the risk of being blown sky-high with the fire-ship attached to us, to divert somewhat the flames which were on the point of reaching the forward powder-magazine. The Master Gunner, who had foreseen the same danger, arrived at this moment to seek my orders on flooding the powder-store, but my reply was negative. I repeated over and over again: 'Long live the King!' – and the cry was enthusiastically taken up by the crew. They were no longer mere men but lions that I had the honour to command! Seeing they were prepared to go down with their ship, I gave orders to fight on to the end. Having succeeded almost miraculously in detaching the fire-ship and sinking it, I took up a position from which the 'Scipion' could retaliate upon the enemy ships which were concentrated against her."

Fig. 121. The battle of Navarino.

The young cadet Harry Codrington, son of the admiral, wrote a letter to his brother, in which he said:

"The 'Asia' had 8 round shot in her bowsprit, 18 in the foremast, 25 mainmast, mizen-mast dowsed, standing and running rigging cut to pieces, lower yards useless, etc., and 125 round shot in the hull, besides quantities of grape, canister, and musket shot, etc.

I had nearly forgotten to tell you how astonished I was at the coolness and intrepidity shown by all the men during the action; and for my part, I was hopping about here and there and everywhere, hurrying them on, for I had not that cool way at all.

A piece of the small upright bars of the iron stern railing of the Admiral's cabin (which had by mistake been left open) was struck by a shot and sent edgeways quite through the calf of my right leg, as I was looking aft; it grazed the shin bone on the inside, and turning clear of it, passed through, tearing a little of the muscle out. In the thigh of the same leg, a little above the knee, a musket ball, or small canister of that size, went in and took a bend clear of the bone, and the deuce knows where it is gone. It must be in, but as it has given me no annoyance and has all but healed up, I am quite content. Then I had a splinter which struck my left collar-bone, and luckily, instead of breaking it, only dislocated it, making a yellow place as big as my two hands put together, but except the bruise, that gave me no pain, and is now all right. I was struck in several other places by splinters, but they were too small to hurt. I went down to the cockpit about the middle of the action. On going down the ladder (tarpaulin and grating being lifted) I found myself almost in the dark and in an atmosphere which was as hot, though not so pure, as many an oven. [Here lay] the wounded, some too bad to speak, others groaning and crying out with the agony they were in. Some (generally the least hurt) calling out lustily for the doctor... I managed to feel my way to an unoccupied birth amidships, alongside a poor fellow who had been severely wounded, and I think we made a pretty quiet pair, except occasional, nay frequent, calls for water." (Woodhouse, op.cit., p. 122)

The battle of Navarino made a great impression amongst Europeans of professed philhellene sentiments. The echo of the stirring conflict was expressed in the following lines by Victor Hugo:

For six years now barbarian Asia
has flooded the wretched land
whose children, few but brave
take no account of life.
Years that have seen Ibrahim
with his repute for insatiable slaughter
fall on the Peloponnese like
the wild goat, where he finds plunder to seize:
villages to uproot and destroy
and when this land is dried up
to send, as proof of the massacre,
heads as gifts to the seraglio.

....

Look, yards are tangling with yards
axes with long burning brands.
all mightily striking and being struck.
Charon stands on the back of the ocean!
How black the slaughter! How great the axe!
The ships, war camps on the water,
with a thousand cannon wounded for ever,

with the troops and sailors broken,
sink and descend to the watery depths.
....
The evil Turk is destroyed,
Greece is free and with songs of joy
Byron in his grave is hymning Navarino.

(Victor Hugo, Navarin, *Les Orientales*, Athens 1921)

The defeat of the Turkish-Egyptian fleet at Navarino signalled the liberation of Greece from Turkish domination and opened the way for the creation of the modern Greek state.

"An untoward event" was how the king of England described the battle, in an attempt to account for the unplanned, chance engagement. But who can isolate chance events in the history of a people that had shed its blood copiously in the struggle for liberation, and had for the previous seven years, from 1821 to 1827, fought and sacrificed everything over the length and breadth of Greece in its fight for national redemption?

The battle of Navarino was one of those paradoxical, but by no means rare, moments in European history when long-standing enemies come together, form an alliance, and fight side by side before quarrelling and coming into conflict with each other once more. Quite apart from – and to some extent independently of – the political and diplomatic agreements, contradictions may be seen in the crews of the three European fleets: the Russians forgot the bestial acts of the French of the Grand Army, which reached and captured Moscow; the French sailors forgot that Codrington, the head of the allied fleet, was a captain of the British fleet at Trafalgar, or that Napoleon's dream had been shattered by the British only twelve years previously at Waterloo; and that the Russians, along with the Prussians and Austrians, had captured Paris in 1815.

Amidst the tissue of political and economic interests, one major contradiction was that in this battle the French played their part in the destruction of the Egyptian fleet which, like the Egyptian army, they had effectively modernised and which was manned by French officers at all levels of the military hierarchy.

For reasons of its own foreign – anti-British – policy, the French government was in favour of staffing the Egyptian army and fleet with French officers, thanks to whom the Egyptian army, before though especially after the Napoleonic Wars, had ceased to consist of savage hordes relying on their religious fanaticism; it was now a well-organised army with excellently trained lancers who obeyed military commands.

And the greatest contradiction of all: Russia, Britain, and France, by participating in the battle of Navarino and crushing the Turkish-Egyptian fleet, contributed to the creation of the modern Greek state; yet these three, along with Austria and Prussia, were members of the Holy Alliance formed by the ruling houses of Europe in 1815, immediately after Waterloo, with the aim of supporting each other in the maintenance of their power and the crushing of any form of national liberation movement.

Directly after the battle, the Messsenian and Lakonian chieftains, their moral renewed, began to mobilise. Theodoros Kolokotronis organised Greek revolutionary movements in the Peloponnese in the light of the new situation. The letter he wrote a few days after the battle to a chieftain at Georgitsi, near Sparta, is indicative:

Fig. 122. Theodoros Kolokotronis (1770-1843), general and commander-in-chief during the Greek War of Independence.

"Dear general captain Panayiotis Papathanassopoulos

It has become incontrovertibly clear that our standards are protected by the almighty Saviour of the nations. The Turkish fleet no longer exists. The invincible fleets of our generous allies have burned it. We too must make a move, in accordance with our national character, to show ourselves worthy of the high opinion that the Christian kings hold of us, and of our expected fortune. The commander-in-chief [Dimitrios Ypsilandis] *has taken drastic measures with regard to the movement of the military forces of Greece, especially those of the Peloponnese. You will be very well informed of this from the enclosed copies of his orders to me, and from his encyclical instructions that he wishes you to communicate to all the villages. I can only follow as closely as possible what he orders, and to this end, I have ordered the generals V. Petimezas, Meletopoulos, Sisinis and Koumaniotis to hasten at his orders to Patra, where he is assembling his camp. Koliopoulos and Gennaios are to go to those parts, that is to say, Messenia, where I intend to go. I have ordered Tziokris, Zapheiropoulos, the Prastiotes and Monemvasiotes to gather at Tripolitza.*

When you receive this letter, you are ordered to mobilise the forces of Yiorgitzi and other villages (send the enclosed on at once) and to go to Kerasies, to where I have also ordered General Petros Barbitziotis to proceed, with the weaponry, and you will wait there until further orders from me, keeping me informed through your reports. You are to attend to food supplies for the soldiers from the villages, until they arrive from the Government, because, for the present, they cannot be provided.

The slightest neglect or indifference on your part will be an unforgivable crime; it may be accounted treason; and your penalty will be expulsion from labouring for the fatherland. I await your answer as soon as possible in Karytaina, where I am going tomorrow; there I shall be in a better position to give orders about your provinces. You must move.

24th October 1827 Valtesinikos
The General commander
of the Peloponnesian armies
Th. Kolokotronis"

(I. Papathanassopoulos, Η ναυμαχία του Ναβαρίνου, *Ιστορία* 112, Athens 1977)

GENERAL MAISON

Fig. 123. The French general Nicholas-Joseph Maison (1770-1841).

After the battle of Navarino, the Turkish Egyptians remained in control of the castles of Messenia for a further year, until September 1828. As soon as Ibrahim left the Peloponnese, the castles were surrendered in the first two weeks of September to the French expeditionary force sent by the Great Powers to Navarino. The king of France, Charles I, assigned command of the expeditionary force to the experienced and courageous general Nicholas-Joseph Maison. Maison had distinguished himself for his military abilities at Flery, Austerlitz (December 1805), and in the campaign against Prussia, had fought in Spain, Holland and Russia, and had been with the last remnants of the Grand Army during Napoleon's retreat from Moscow.

The French expeditionary force disembarked at Petalidi, where it stayed for a while before pitching camp at Yialova, the coastal area at the head of the bay of Navarino. The installation here of the expeditionary force proved to be a disaster for the French soldiers, for in September and October 1828 the men in the camp were afflicted by a fever, as a result of which 4,760 of a total of 13,760 men fell sick and 915 died.

Fig. 124. French soldiers landing in Messenia.

Fig. 125. The large plain of Yialova with Divari and, in the background, the Sykia strait between Koryphasion and Sphakteria. On this plain, so charged with memories of Mycenaean times, the Classical period, and the Second Venetian period, Ibrahim and Maison inspected the French expeditionary corps just before the former left Greece forever in defeat.

Fig. 126. Nikitas Stamatelopoulos (1787-1849), also known as Nikitaras. Stamatelopoulos was military governor of Messenia and fought alongside of Kolokotronis, whose nephew he was.

Fig. 127. Ibrahim and Maison meet at Yialova.
Maison had invited Ibrahim, and also Derigny, Heyden and other European officers to review the French expeditionary force in training (October 1828). Nikitaras was also present at the ceremony reaffirming friendly relations between Egypt and France.

THE MAISON BARRACKS IN NIOKASTRO

After the departure of the Turkish Egyptians, the first and main concern of the French expeditionary force was to undertake extensive repairs to and renovation of the fortification walls and bastions at Niokastro and the fort of Methone. At the same time, maintenance work was carried out on the aqueduct at Pylos, the new road from Pylos to Methone was laid out, paved, and converted into a motor road, and the modern, new town of Pylos was designed and built. One important aspect of the expeditionary force's activity was the organising of the "Expédition Scientifique de Morée" by archaeologists, architects, and historians. The French scholars catalogued, drew and described the major ancient monuments of the Peloponnese and surrounding area, thereby providing valuable evidence for modern historians.

The building in the town known as the Dioikitirio (administrative headquarters) and the Maison Barracks in Niokastro are also the work of the French. The barracks, a plain, stone, rectangular, two-storey building measuring 47 × 16 m. and covered by a pitched roof, stands just inside the north entrance to the fortress. The upper storey of the building is reached by two exterior stone staircases at either end of the long east side. The purpose to which the building was put after the departure of the French is unknown. It may be regarded as certain, however, that it was occupied by soldiers when the fortress was used as a training centre for cadets of the newly formed Greek state; and that it later served as an administrative building for the gendarmerie, after the citadel in the fortress had been converted into a prison for long-term convicts. From the end of the Second World War until 1982 the Barracks was used by the Archaeological Service as a storeroom and laboratory for the conservation of antiquities.

Fig. 128. General Maison's administrative headquarters in Pylos on the day it was demolished in November 1986.

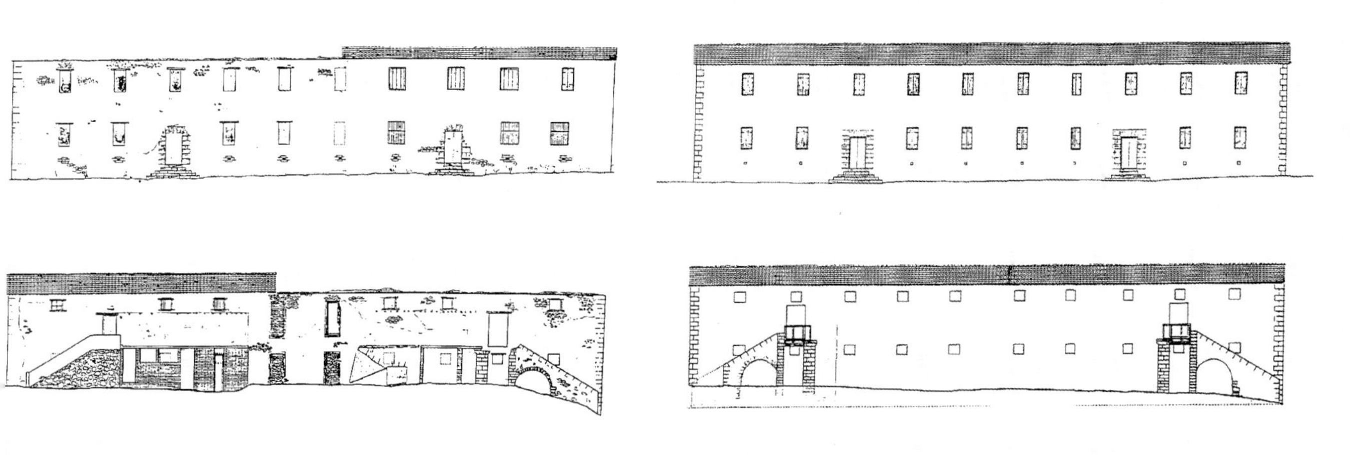

Fig. 129. The Maison Barracks. Measured drawings and reconstruction drawing of the west and east facades.

NIOKASTRO, A PRISON FOR LONG-TERM CONVICTS

After the creation of the Greek state, Niokastro became a military base and was used until 1864 as a cadet training centre. It was then converted for many years into a prison, a fate it shared with most castles in Greece.

Political foes of the authorities interned in the fortress, and criminals, often serving long sentences, including those under sentence of death, lived in awful, inhuman conditions in Niokastro. Before Niokastro was used as a prison, the necessary structural modifications were made to the citadel. To create cells for the prisoners, all the vaults supporting the passageways were blocked up by a wall. The large vaulted room on the north side of the citadel, beneath the ramp, was also converted into accommodation for prisoners, as were the two spacious rooms in bastion V. For reasons of security and control, the large interior courtyard of the citadel on to which all the cells looked, was divided into five areas by radially placed partition walls. These partition walls originally consisted of railings, until quarrels and conflicts between prisoners became too intense, when the railings had to be replaced by high walls.

Fig. 130-131. Characteristic views of cells in the prison on the east side of the citadel before the renovation of the fortress in 1982-1984.

The prison kitchen was immediately to the left of the entrance to the citadel, and makeshift stone wash-houses were constructed above the cistern in the courtyard. The toilets were built in a vault next to bastion II, which was known as the "Arab". To assist with control of the prisoners, the two staircases in the citadel were sealed and a small guardhouse was built on the flat roof of bastion V. The prison in Niokastro functioned up to the early 1950s, despite the fact that its use was officially forbidden in 1936.

The wretched living conditions for the prisoners are described by René Puaux: *"The prisoners held in Navarino, who are true criminals, undeserving of sympathy ... play cards by day or walk in the interior courtyard which is partitioned off by railings and encircled on high by the path used by the night patrol, reminding one of a bear-pit in a zoo. These wretches beg for drachmas from visitors, just as the animals of Berne raise their noses to get carrots. When Henrie Belle (First Secretary at the French embassy), who visited Greece in the 1860s, came here, about fifteen of the inmates danced a very lively 'kalamatianos', despite the heavy chains around their ankles ... They go around, alone or in pairs in the confined space, with the mournful submission of harmless lunatics. One of the condemned who was shut up in his cell was throwing crumbs of bread through the bars to the birds that had flocked in front of him."*

Fig. 132. Niokastro. Citadel. The prison courtyard with its high radial walls; these were demolished in 1983 during the renovation of the fortress.

Fig. 133. Niokastro. Convicts in the citadel prison.

Fig. 134. Niokastro. Citadel. The radial walls of the prison and the guard-house in bastion V; these were demolished in 1984 during the renovation of the fortress.

RENÉ PUAUX

Fig. 135. René Puaux (1878-1936).

René Puaux, who was closely associated with Greece and Pylos, has been described as the last French philhellene.

He made it his life's work to collect works of art of the period of philhellenism, and in 1935 held an exhibition of his collection in Paris under the title "Philhellénisme", to honour of the struggles of Greece and his compatriots who had supported those struggles. He donated his collection – mainly engravings, documents and souvenirs of the War of Independence – to Pylos, believing that this was its proper place. René Puaux died in Paris in 1936.

Ten years after his death, the Greek author Kazantzakis wrote of the great 20th century philhellene:

"René Puaux was born in 1878 to a select Protestant family, and was the son and grandson of pastors. He began to write at an early age. Handsome, strong, full of the love of life, all finesse and humour, he wrote verses, travelled to Britain, fell in love with the British poets, wrote a book called 'British Silhouettes', returned to France and entered the powerful family of editors of the Temps, a newspaper of worldwide repute. René Puaux was dissipating himself, his life had not yet acquired any central core that would satisfy and assimilate all his desires and abilities, when suddenly his newspaper sent him as a war correspondent to cover the First Balkan War. From then onwards, René Puaux's life acquired a unity, found a purpose, became connected with a great idea: he became acquainted and fell in love with modern Greece.

'I shall remain true to Greece, I shall remain true to Greece in her joy and in her grief', proclaimed René Puaux. He stood firmly by this oath he swore to himself until the end of his life. Out of fervent love, out of lucid understanding, out of a profound conviction that by serving the idea of Greece he was serving mankind.

He travelled widely in the mountains and islands of Greece, got to know the landsmen and sailors at close quarters, and loved modern Greece as few other foreigners have – not as a reflection of ancient Greece, but for its own sake, with all its modern eccentricities, with the great virtues of the Greek people – their native wit, industriousness, hospitality, love of travel and adventure, their burning love for their country...".

(Paris 22.12. 1946, *Νέα Εστία* 41 (1947), p. 71)

THE GREEK CENTRE OF UNDERWATER ARCHAEOLOGY AT PYLOS

During the five years from 1982 to 1987, there was a thoroughgoing renovation of Niokastro as part of a programme designed by the Ephorate of Underwater Archaeology, which envisaged the institution, establishment, and functioning in the castle of the Greek Centre of Underwater Archaeology at Pylos.

As part of the programme, the renovated areas of the prison, the cells, the bastions and the castle vaults, are used as offices, laboratories for the conservation of antiquities, and archaeological storerooms. One large room, the entrance to which is beneath the citadel ramp, has been converted into a hall for conferences, lectures, temporary exhibitions, music concerts, performances of plays and the screening of films.

In accordance with the plan for the renovation of the fortress for the needs of the Greek Centre of Underwater Archaeology, the Maison Barracks building was consolidated and restored in 1984 on the basis of an archaeological study by the present writer.

The ground floor of the building has been redesigned to house the Pylos Art Gallery, the core of which is the René Puaux collection, and guest quarters consisting of five rooms have been created on the upper storey for the needs of the Centre. A library has also been formed, to which the publisher Notis Karavias has donated his extensive private collection, which includes old newspapers and a variety of publications, periodicals and books dealing with the modern history of Pylos and the Peloponnese.

Fig. 136. Niokastro. Citadel. The multi-purpose room before the restoration of the fortress.

Fig. 137. Niokastro. Citadel. The multi-purpose room of the Pylos Centre of Underwater Archaeology.
This room was originally an ammunition magazine, and therefore had no windows, apart from ventilation holes. The two large side windows were created so that it could be used by convicts.

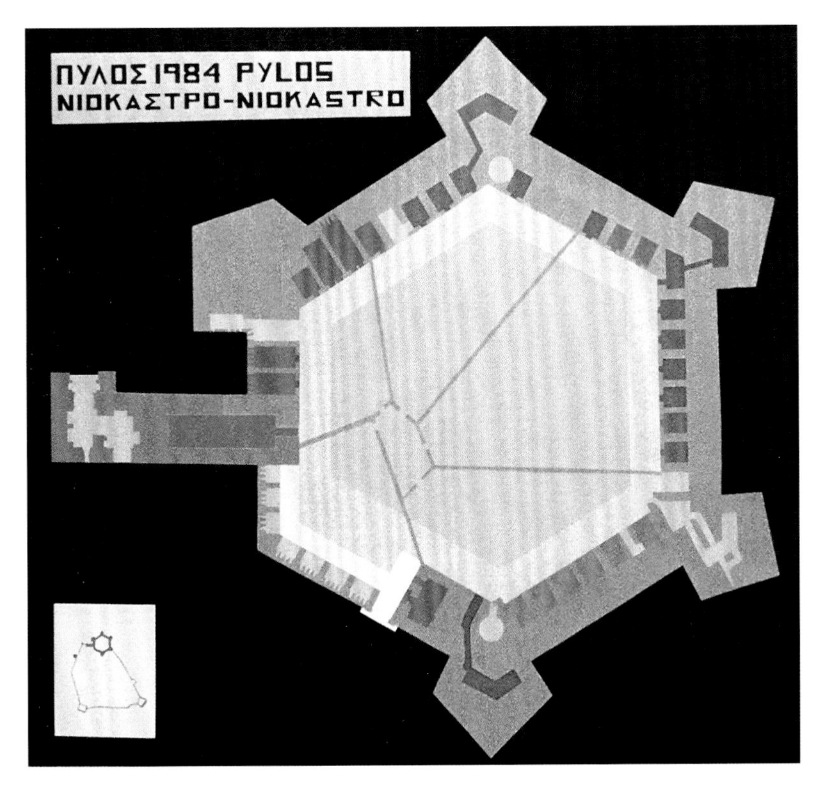

Fig. 138. The poster of the Third International Conference on Underwater Archaeology. Pylos, summer 1984.

Fig. 139-140. Niokastro. The Maison Barracks. The south-west part of the barracks before and after the building was renovated to serve as the Pylos Art Gallery.

Fig. 141. Niokastro. The Maison Barracks. Interior of the upper storey after the renovation work of 1982-1984.

Fig. 142. Niokastro. The Maison Barracks after the renovation. East facade.

MODERN PYLOS AND THE EARLY MODERN MONUMENTS OF NAVARINO

During the Turkish period, Niokastro was occupied by Turks, while the Greek population was concentrated outside the fortress at modern Kalyvia, formerly known as Varousi. Varousi is a word of Slav origin used by the Turks to describe the Christian communities that resided outside their settlements. The French of the expeditionary force developed the small, insignificant Greek settlement into a town based on a spacious, rectangular public square enclosed by a portico for the needs of the market. The form and basic tissue of the new town – austere and functional, yet charming – are still virtually unchanged.

According to the testimony of William Leake, who visited Messenia at the beginning of the 19th century, there were 300 Turkish families living in Niokastro. Over the entire area enclosed by the outer wall of Niokastro, there are visible remains on either side of the streets of the Turkish settlement.

Fig. 143. Niokastro and the surrounding area showing the position of the old Greek settlement to the north-east of the castle.

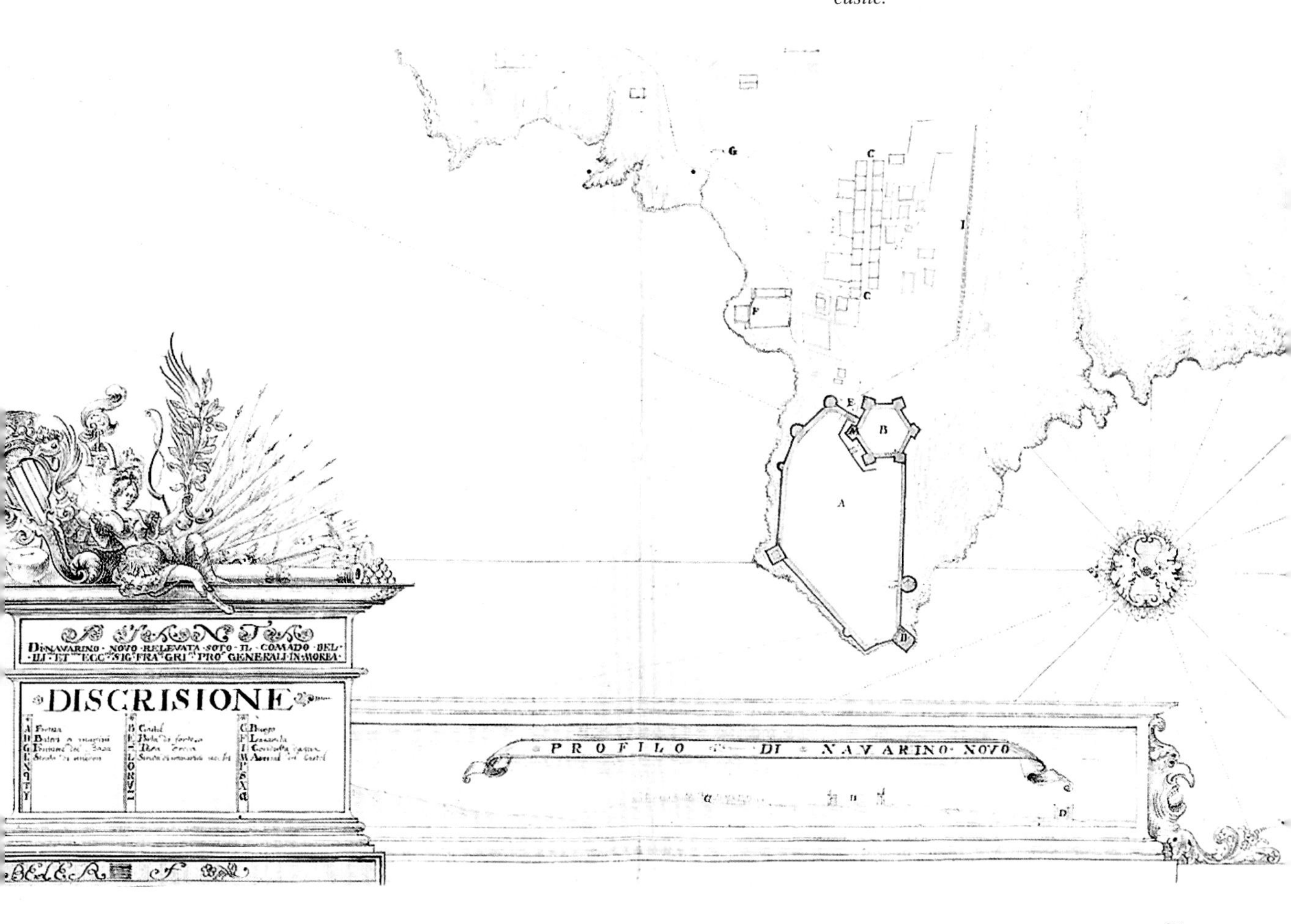

Fig. 144. Konstantinos Tsiklitiras (1888-1913), the Olympic gold-medallist.

In the late 19th and early 20th century, roadworks were carried out on the seafront, sewers were laid, a breakwater 110 m. long was constructed, a dock was constructed at the harbour, pipes were laid to carry water from Koumbes (1905-1909), and the harbour was deepened.

The monument to the three admirals, a three-sided marble structure each side of which depicts one of the three admirals who fought at the battle of Navarino in 1827, was executed in 1933 by the sculptor Thomas Thomopoulos of Smyrna and now stands in the Trion Navarchon Square. To the right and left of the monument are a Venetian and a Turkish cannon, brought here from Niokastro.

The house of the Olympic gold-medallist Konstantinos Tsiklitiras is preserved at Pylos. Tsiklitiras won his medal in the standing long-jump at the Stockholm Olympics in 1912.

Fig. 145. Pylos in 1927.

Fig. 146. The Russian monument on the east coast of Sphakteria.

The monument of the Unknown Soldier, carved by the sculptor Karachalios, stands in front of the Town Hall of Pylos.

The Pylos Archaeological Museum was built thanks to the generosity of the Messenian doctor Christos Antonopoulos. It houses archaeological finds from Pylia, mainly from the Mycenaean tombs at Koukounara (excavations by Sp. Marinatos) and the Hellenistic tumulus at Tsopani Rachi (excavations by G. Papathanassopoulos).

On Tsichli-Baba, the rocky islet at the south end of Sphakteria, is a monument honouring the French officers and soldiers killed during the battle of Navarino. It is the work of C. Troum and was erected in 1890. The monument to the Russians lost in the battle was placed on Sphakteria itself, near the old chapel of the Panagoula, which was destroyed during the events of 1825. The British monument stands on the rocky islet of Chelonaki in the bay.

There is also a pyramidal gravestone on Sphakteria for Alexis Males, one of Maison's officers who was killed in a duel in 1833, and a monument to Paul-Marie Bonaparte, Napoleon's nephew. At the age of eighteen, the young Bonaparte enrolled as a volunteer on the frigate of the British admiral Cochrane, under captain Andreas Miaoulis, and was killed on board ship while cleaning his weapon.

The most recent monument to be erected on Sphakteria, in 1959, is devoted to the memory of those who lost their lives in 1825, during Ibrahim's raid.

Fig. 147. The French monument on the high Tsichli-Baba rock that dominates the entrance to the bay.

Fig. 148. The British monument on the rocky islet of Chelonaki in the middle of the bay.

MOTHOCORONA, "THE EYES OF VENICE"

The east has grown rosy, the west become light
the mountains are full of dew and the orange-trees of flowers.
The heaven has shown signs, the armada is coming
with sixty-five galleys and sixty-two frigates
and they are going to take Mothone and Corone.
- Mothone, give us the keys, Corone, surrender.
- I am not Patras that you can scare me, Vostitsa to quake in fear
I am Corone the famous, Mothone the much-praised;
and I have the youths of Corone, all of them brave young warriors,
who hold their swords in their teeth, their rifles in their hands
I can withstand war for forty-five years!

Folk song about the war between the Venetians and the Turks during the campaign to capture the Peloponnese in 1685. (Dim. A. Petropoulos, Ιστορικά δημοτικά τραγούδια της Πελοποννήσου, *Πελοποννησιακά* 1 (1956), p. 164-165)

METHONE

Methone is identified by Strabo (*Geography* 8, 359-360) and Pausanias (*Messeniaka* IV, 35, 1) with Homer's Pedasos, one of the seven cities presented by Agamemnon to Achilles to appease his anger and persuade him to return to battle (*Iliad* IX, 294). In ancient times it was referred to as Mothone, the name that is also inscribed on its coins.

After the Spartan victory in the Second Messenian War, many of the inhabitants of Methone migrated to Kyllene, along with the inhabitants of Pylos. Those that stayed behind became helots. The Athenians attempted to capture Methone during the Peloponnesian War, in 431, six years before they came to Pylos. They failed to detach it from the Spartans, however, on account of the decisive, lightning intervention by the brilliant Spartan general Brasidas. In his account of this episode, Thucydides states (II, 25, translated by Rex Warner, Penguin edition):

"Meanwhile the Athenian fleet of 100 ships which was sailing round the Peloponnese continued on its voyage. The Athenians had been reinforced by fifty ships from Corcyra and others from their allies in that area. After doing damage at various places they landed in Spartan territory at Methone and made an attack on the fortifications there, which were weak and had been left without a garrison. However, Brasidas, the son of Tellis, a Spartan officer, happened to be in this district with a special detachment of men. When he realized what was happening he came to the support of the defenders of the place with 100 hoplites. Finding the Athenian army dispersed over the country and with its attention occupied on the fortifications, he charged right through it and forced his way into Methone, losing a few of his

men in the action, but saving the city. Because of this exploit, he was the first person in the war to receive official congratulations at Sparta."

It is thus clear that at the time of the Peloponnesian War, there was a fortified city at the harbour. The extent of the ancient fortifications is unknown, however, since the earlier material was reused in the numerous later repairs and extensions, leading to the disappearance almost all traces of the original structure.

In 354 BC, Methone was captured by Philip II, and in 191 BC it joined the Achaian Confederacy.

Pausanias records that there were temples of Athena Anemotis and Artemis at Methone, and also a well from which issued water and tar (*Μεσσηνιακά* IV, 35, 8), though none of these have yet been located.

From the 4th c. AD onwards, this important commercial harbour also became a supply station for warships and rapidly came to occupy a position of importance for Byzantine shipping. The Early Christian burials and the rock-cut arcosolia at Ayios Onouphrios near Methone (possibly 4th c.), taken together with the fact that Methone is mentioned as early as 386 as a staging post on the sea route from Italy to Constantinople, confirm that the region had not been abandoned at this date and attest to the early conversion of the inhabitants to the new

Fig. 149. Aerial photograph of Methone. The traces of the old streets in the fortress can be seen, and also the ancient mole, now beneath the sea.

religion. The Byzantine scholar D. Pallas asserts that the complex of rock-cut tombs at Ayios Onouphrios had several points of similarity with the Early Christian catacombs of Southern Italy and Sicily. Pallas considers it reasonable that the tombs would have been influenced by the funerary architecture of Southern Italy, given the relations that existed at the time between the Italian coast and Methone.

In 533, the warships of Belisarius, Justinian's general, are said to have anchored in the harbour of Methone during his campaign against the Vandals in North Africa.

In 881, the Byzantine fleet sailed to Methone and went on to defeat the Arab fleet at Zakynthos. Before returning to Constantinople, the Byzantine admiral, Nasar, returned to Methone and presented the Arab ships he had captured to the church there. In the 11th c., the Greeks appealed to the Venetians for aid in dealing with the Normans who were threatening the Byzantine empire. The Venetians responded, but in return secured privileges for the movement of Venetian merchandise. The year 1082 marked the beginning of Venetian rule at Methone.

In 1125, the Doge Domenico Michielli, who was known as *Terror Graecorum* (the terror of the Greeks) launched a counter-attack against Ioannis II Komninos, the Byzantine emperor, who was disputing the privileges ceded to the Venetians by his father Alexios I.

Michielli landed at Methone, which had been captured by the Byzantines, and razed the town to the ground. The Byzantines not only failed to restrict the trading privileges granted to the Venetians but were obliged to ratify and renew them in 1126, 1148, 1187, and 1199.

When, therefore, Constantinople was captured by the Franks (1204) and the crusaders divided the territories of the empire amongst themselves, Methone might have been expected to be granted to the Venetians. However, the division *(partitio Romaniae)* agreed between the

Fig. 150. Ayios Onouphrios. Early Christian cemetery cut into the rock in the side of a hill 2 km. north of Methone, on the left of the road to Pylos. In the Byzantine period it was converted into a retreat of the same name.

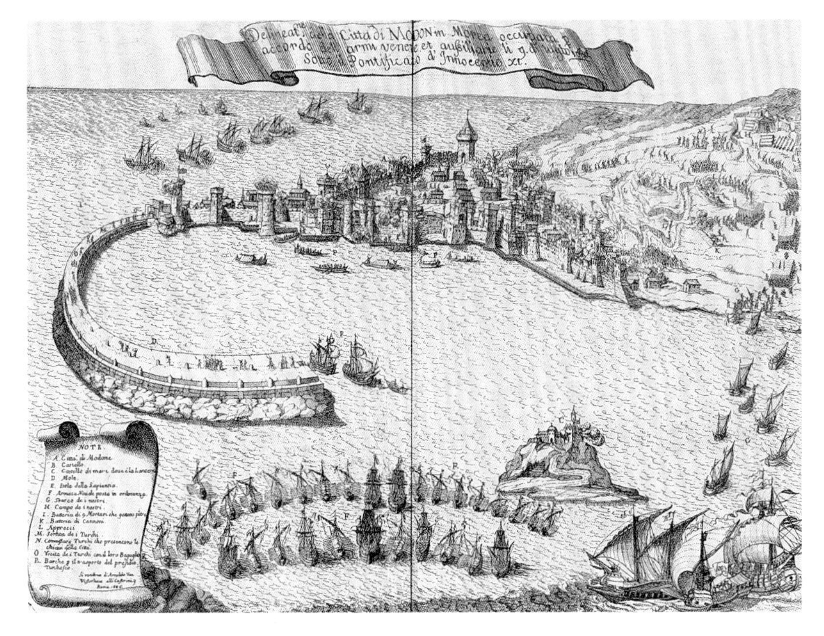

Fig. 151. The fortress and harbour of Methone.
The last Byzantine emperor to call in at Methone was Ioannis VIII Palaiologos, who was travelling with the patriarch Joseph II and his retinue for the Council of Ferrara-Florence. This council was also attended by Pope Eugenios IV, and dealt with the question of the unification of the Churches and common action against the Ottoman Turks.
In the illustration, the Latin church dedicated to Saint John the Theologian can be seen to the left of the main large tower. On 23 November 1439 the emperor Ioannis VIII Palaiologos attended a service in this church when he called at Methone on his way back to Constantinople after the Council of Ferrara-Florence.

conquerors had a largely theoretical character, since the Franks and Venetians had not actually captured any territory outside Constantinople itself. The next rulers of Methone were therefore to be, for three years, the Franks, led by Geoffrey Villehardouin, nephew of Geoffrey Villehardouin who was one of the leaders of the Crusaders who captured Constantinople, and at the same time a chronicler of the conquest:

"It chanced that Geoffrey de Villehardouin, the nephew of Geoffrey the marshal of Romania and Champagne, having departed from Syria with those who had recently arrived at Constantinople was driven by the winds and waves into Modon. The injury sustained by his ship compelled him to winter in the country; which coming to the ears of a Greek who was a powerful lord of the country, he sought him and having treated him with much distinction, addressed him in these terms: 'Fair sir, the Franks have subdued the city of Constantinople and have made one of themselves emperor. If you are inclined to bear me company, I will observe good faith towards you, and we will possess ourselves of much of the territory in this neighbourhood...' They entered by oath into this fellowship and subdued together much of the Morea; and Geoffrey de Villehardouin had no cause to complain of the good faith of the Greek. But it pleased God that the Greek fell sick and died; and his son, turning against Geoffrey de Villehardouin, proved a traitor to him and seduced his castles and garrisons to declare against him. Geoffrey, having heard that the marquis [...] with a great force was besieging Napoli, in the course of six days, though with great danger, traversed the country and arrived at the camp, where he was honourably received by the marquis and his friends. And this honourable reception was his due; for he was noble and valiant, and a knight of unblemished fame.

The marquis would have assigned him land and subsistence to induce

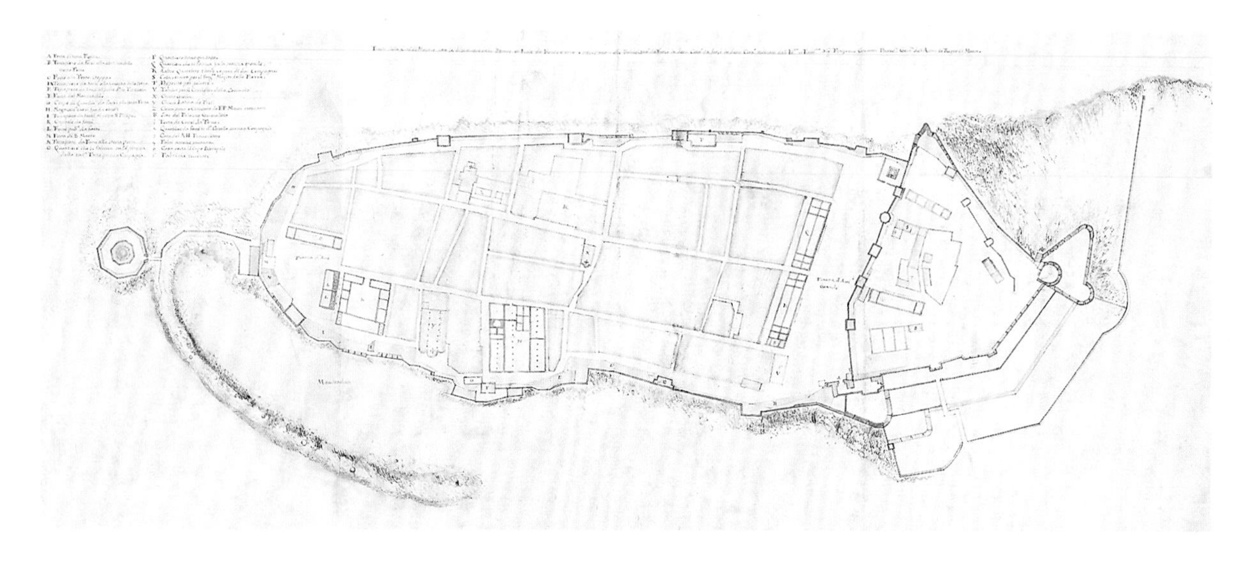

Fig. 152. The fortress of Methone. Drawing made by the Venetians before 1714.
The fortress had one gate on the land side (Porta di Terra Ferma A), three on the sea side, two of them to the east (Porta Stoppa C and Porta di Mandrachin F) and one to the south (Porta di San Marco M). The two to the east were used mainly for loading and unloading merchandise on ships, and that at the south communicated with the Bourtzi. All the gates had portcullises. The drawing shows the street network of the settlement; this was once covered with ruins but has now largely been uncovered.

him to continue in his service, but he would accept nothing; and seeking William de Champlitte, who was his intimate friend, he said, 'Sir, I come from a rich country called the Morea; take as many followers as you can command and leave the camp; and by God's grace we will go and conquer that country. And whatever portion of the spoil it shall please you to assign to me, I will hold of you, and therefore become your liegeman.' As William de Champlitte loved and believed Geoffrey de Villehardouin, he immediately sought the marquis and submitted the proposal to him, who permitted him to undertake the enterprise. So William de Champlitte and Geoffrey de Villehardouin, with about a hundred men at arms and a great number of sergeants on horseback, left the camp and, entering the Morea, marched to the city of Modon.

Michael, being advised that they had entered the country with no great strength, raised a marvellous great army and hastened after them, as if he thought they were already in his toils. When they heard of his approach, they repaired the fortifications of Modon, which had been long dismantled; and there leaving their baggage and helpless people, they marched out and drew up their army with all the force they could number; not without danger, for they had only five hundred horsemen, while the enemy numbered five thousand. But as God governs all things, they gave battle to the Greeks, who were defeated and dispersed with great slaughter. The French gained horses, arms, and other property in abundance, with which they returned gaily and joyously to the city of Modon.

They afterwards besieged a city on the sea shore called Coron; which, after a short resistance, was surrendered. Upon this capture, William de Champlitte bestowed the city on Geoffrey de Villehardouin."

(Geoffrey Villehardouin, *The Conquest of Constantinople,* London 1829, § 330)

The clash between the Greeks and Franks at Kountoura – the only set battle between the foes that was not connected with a siege or the capture of a castle – is described in the *Chronicle of the Morea* (ll. 1690-1738):

"Thereon they fitted out the ships and went straightway to Methon. They found the castle deserted, it was completely destroyed, the Venetians had destroyed it earlier, because the [Greeks] used to keep their ships there and had been stopping and looting ships of the Venetians. And then they set out and went to the castle of Korone, and they found the castle with low walls and towers; it lay upon a precipitous crag and was fortified; but the ships encircled it all around. The knights and the foot soldiers began the battle; they set up the trebuchets and shot repeatedly at them therein; indeed those Koronians who were inside the castle had no possibility whatever to stand upon the walls; seeing the multitude of troops and the boldness of the attack, they cried out and asked that they be pardoned, that they would surrender the castle to them, with the proviso that they would swear to them that they would have their houses and likewise their patrimonies. The marshal Sir Geoffrey heard this; quickly he promised them; the battle was stilled; the Franks entered within and received the castle; they placed provisions within and troops of their own, and on the following day they set out and went to Kalamata. They found the castle dilapidated, it was being used as a monastery: arriving before it, they attacked it and took it by the sword; the defenders surrendered it on terms, as the others had done.

Now, as soon as the [Greeks] in Nikli, those of Veligosti, and those of Lakedaemonia learned of it, they all gathered together, foot soldiers and knights; their foot soldiers came from the defiles of the Melings; they came from the villages of Lakkos and arrived at Chrysorea, where they heard and learned that the Franks had come, and they marched our from the villages and began to plunder and said and planned that they would defeat them. They were led to the place called Kapeskianous, to a spot which bears the name 'at the olive grove of Kountoura'. There were four thousand of them, foot soldiers and knights. Now, when the Franks learned of this, again from the [Greeks] who were with them and who knew the land, they led them there and they went and found them and they waged battle, the Franks and the [Greeks]. And the Franks, foot soldiers and knights, were only 700 in number, so many were they reckoned. The [Greeks] began the battle with eagerness, because they saw them so few; later they repented. Why should I tell you the many details and what would be my gain? The Franks won the battle at that time; they killed them all, few escaped them. That was the only battle that the [Greeks] fought during the time that the Franks conquered Morea."

(*The Chronicle of the Morea,* 1964, p. 118-121)

Fig. 153. Fortress of Methone. Church of Saint Ioannis Theologos. The south-west corner of the church with the base of the minaret, evidence that it was converted into a mosque. The mosque was demolished shortly after Greece won its independence, when the new settlement was founded outside the fortress.

Fig. 154. Fortress of Methone. Church of Saint Ioannis Theologos. The south-west corner of the church after its conversion to a mosque.

Whereas the Frankish Crusaders looked upon Methone and Corone as simply new coastal territories that they had captured, for the Venetians they were the connecting link in a chain of trading posts. The Venetians continued to covet the fine harbours of Methone and Corone and attacked the area in 1207, obliging the Frankish defenders to surrender. From this time until 1500, the Venetians controlled Methone and Corone, which were regarded as the "eyes of Venice", half way along the sea route from Venice to the Holy Land. This route was monopolised by Venetian ships, that put in at Methone and Corone to take on supplies and carry merchandise from the Peloponnese, mainly Messenia, to Venice and Western Europe: salt, silk, wax, grain, and olive oil. The slave trade is also said to have flourished in the slave-markets of Methone and Corone.

Through the possession of Methone, Corone, Nauplion, and Argos, and bases in the Aegean and Ionian seas, Venice had secured for her naval empire an ideal network of trading posts and centres.

The central authority in Venice took care that Methone and Corone were always regularly supplied – with food, munitions and materials – and kept an eye on the functioning of these valuable trading posts.

A good idea of the relations between the centre and the colonies, and of the social life of the latter, is provided by the documents and letters that were constantly being sent to the governors and *provveditori* of the fortresses of Methone and Corone. The following documents form a good example; they are presented "according to the diplomatic method" (G.S. Ploumidis, Συλλογή εγγράφων για τις βενετοκρατούμενες Μεθώνη και Κορώνη, *Πελοποννησιακά* 10 (1974), p. 155-164):

27.7.1465. The new capitaneo and provvisor of Corone Mafeo Leono is to receive wages for six months.

23.1.1466. The ship of Andreas Mauroceno to depart at once for Methone with 2200 "stara" of corn.

8.5.1466. The rectors of Corone are ordered to pay the soldiers regularly. Capitaneo Mafeo Leono should not have been paid his wages in advance while the soldiers remain without wages.

25.8.1466. The [Catholic] inhabitants of Methone have requested that the Dominican monk Aloysius Longo, who is in Methone, be appointed bishop. Action to be taken with the Holy Seat.

19.5.1467. 500 ducats are to be sent to Corone for the repair of the fortification walls that have collapsed as a result of earthquake.

21.9.1467. Corn is to be sent urgently to Methone.

29.7.1469. The authorities at Methone may spend 250 ducats to dredge the harbour.

6.7.1470. A commander of archers is to be sent at once to Methone.

30.10.1470. The engineer Giovanni de la Massa is being sent to Methone to see to the fortifying of the town. He will be paid 200 ducats a year.

13.12.1470. Someone has offered to build hand-operated flour-mills at Methone and Corone, at his own expense, asking only to retain the exclusive use of them for 20 years. Application approved.

2.3.1471. 1000 posts, 200 beams and 200 planks are being sent to Methone to fence in the harbour there.

12.12.1471. The head of the supply service of Methone, Peregrino, is to come to Venice and present his books.

13.8.1472. 500 ducats are being sent to Corone to complete the public warehouse.

3.9.1494. Since the salt lakes at Methone yield little revenue, it is ordered that in future only the local deputato shall sell salt there. From the income from the salt lakes, 200 ducats are to be given to pay the soldiers and 4000 "stara" of millet are to be bought. Any money left over is to be used for the repair of the harbour and the fortification walls.

29.10.1501. The 28 soldiers from Methone and the 30 from Zonchio are to be given land on Kephallinia and an additional grant of 4 ducats a year. They are obliged, however, to maintain a horse.

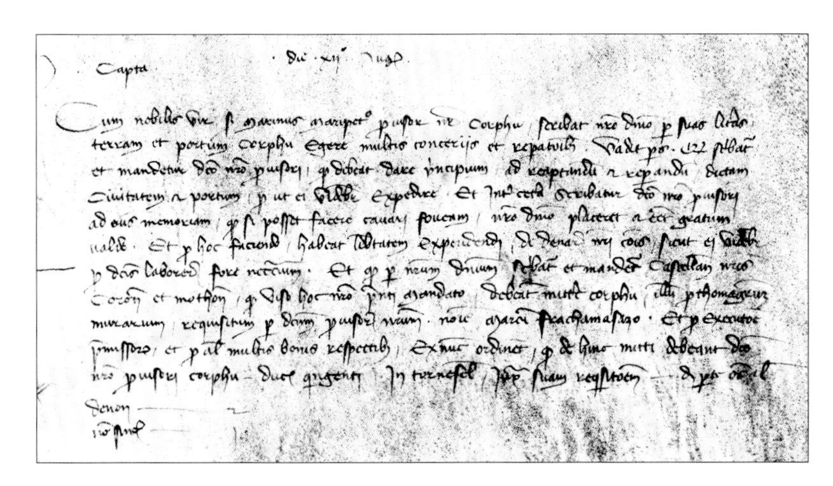

Fig. 155. Commercial letter from the Venetian administration of Corfu to Venice, asking among other things for salt to be sent to Methone and a master-craftsman specialising in fortifications. Salt was a basic item of trade, in which Venice held the monopoly not only in the salt lakes of the Adriatic but also in their possessions in Greece.
The original letter is kept in the Corfu library.

Fig. 156. *Paliomothone. Church of Saint Leo. The preserved north facade, with the interior of the south side of the 15th c. church behind it.*

Fig. 157. *Paliomothone. Church of Saint Leo. Reconstruction drawings of the monument:*
a. Plan of the 13th c. Frankish church.
b-c. Elevation and plan of the 15th c. Venetian church.
The hatched area on the plan is the single-aisled cross-vaulted church of the 15th c.

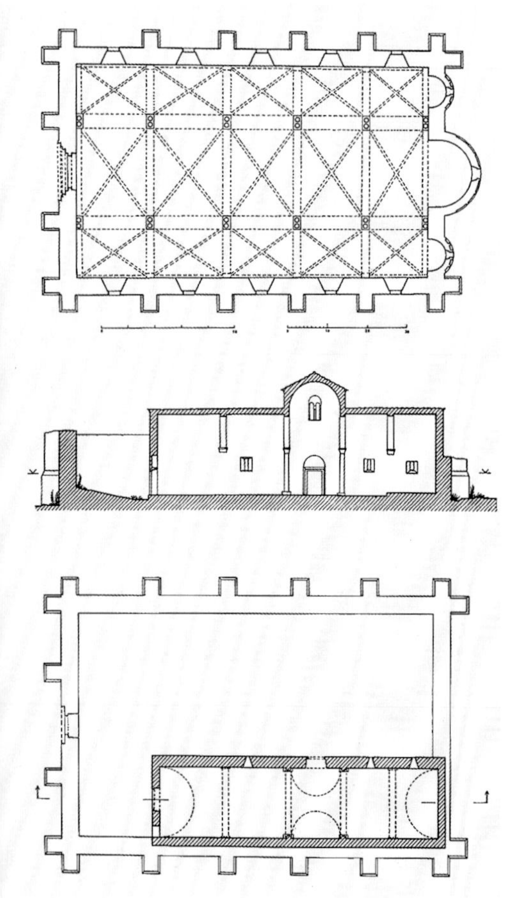

During the ten centuries of the existence of the Byzantine empire, and particularly after the Frankish and Venetian periods, Methone was an essential port of call on the route from Constantinople to the West. In the 15th c., when the Turkish threat was tightening around Byzantium, the emperors set out from Constantinople and called at Methone before going on to the West to ask for help.

Inside the fortress at Methone is a large three-aisled basilica of Saint Ioannis Theologos. It has a timber roof and external buttresses, and reveals the influence of Gothic architecture. When Methone came under Turkish domination, the church of Saint Ioannis was converted into a mosque.

At Paliomothone, about 3 km. to the north-east of the harbour, there was a spacious three-aisled basilica dating from the first half of the 13th c., of which only the outer wall is preserved to a low height. The church, which measured 18.40 × 29.19 m., probably belonged to the order of the Cistercian monks, which was very powerful at this period. This Frankish church appears to have been demolished quite quickly, and the Venetians erected a single-aisled cross-vaulted church on the site about 200 years later, just before they were driven out by Bayezid II. This church was once thought to have been dedicated to the memory of Saint Leo the Young, or the Miracle-worker. However, recent investigations in the archives of Venice and on the building remains, have shown that the church dedicated to Saint Leo, the local saint, should be sought on the coast of the bay of Methone.

Methone, the harbour famed for its wine – Homer's Pedasos rich in vines – and one of the best fortified towns in the Peloponnese, like the Oinouses islands opposite, was for centuries the object of pirate raids, as was the rest of the Peloponnesian coast. The

Fig. 158. Fortress of Methone. The fortifications on the east side.

pirate ships usually lurked behind the Oinouses islands, waiting to attack the Venetian galleys as they left the harbour.

One of the pilgrims who called at Methone on their way to the Holy Land during the 15th c. was Petro Tafur, who came to Methone in 1436 and wrote in his diary that there were 2,000 inhabitants, who lived inside the fortress in good quality houses, with orchards. Another pilgrim, Felix Faber, who stayed here in 1483, was impressed by the thick walls and strong towers.

During the Second Venetian-Turkish War (1499-1503), Venice lost Naupaktos and Lefkada and also her important trading posts of Methone and Corone. In 1500, the second year of the Turkish campaign against the areas occupied by Venice, the sultan Bayezid II captured Methone, which was defended by 7,000 men. The fine

Fig. 159. Fortress of Methone. The Bourtzi: the coastal tower at the south end of the peninsula.
The three-storey tower has a large underground cistern. On the first floor are seventeen cannon emplacements facing the sea and densely set rifle slits only on the side towards the fortress.

Fig. 160. Fortress of Methone. The north end of the west side, where the unfinished moat ends.

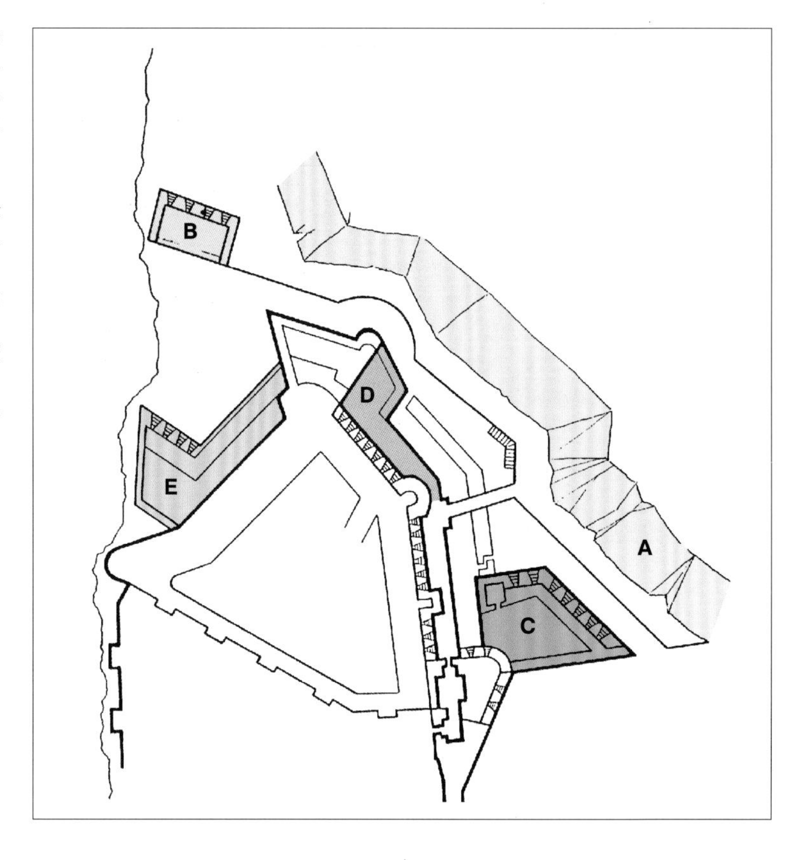

Fig. 161. Fortress of Methone. The defence works carried out on the north side, just before the final departure of the Venetians from the Peloponnese, which are not marked on their plans.
A. Outer face of moat.
B. The "advanced fort" at the vulnerable west end of the moat, showing the south side unwalled.
C. The Loredan bastion, which required a new, straight line for the moat.
D. Retaining wall at the bastion, next to and lower than the Bembo bastion.
E. "Advanced fort" at the moat on the north-west side of the small enclosure.

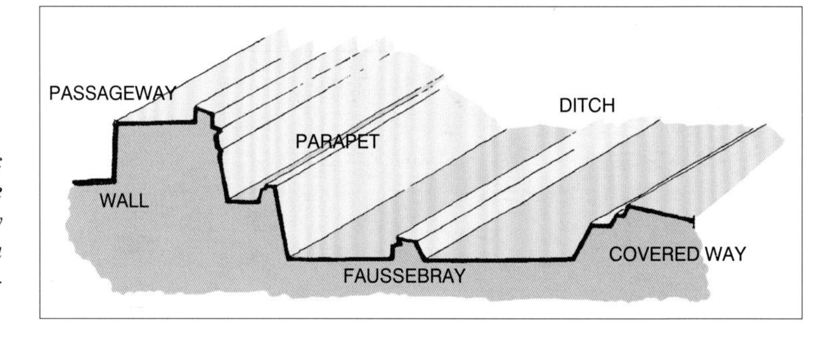

Fig. 162. Fortress of Methone. Schematic transverse section of the defence works on the north-east side, in the form they were finally given by the Venetians up to 1714. Based on a drawing by K. Andrews (Castles of the Morea, NJ 1953, p. 64).

Fig. 163. Fortress of Methone. The south side of the fortress with its imposing gate opposite the Bourtzi, with which it was linked by a bridge.

harbour was besieged by land and sea, by 250 ships and an army of 100,000 men. The Venetian garrison surrendered after three months of siege, which was accompanied by continual, remorseless cannon bombardment. The surrender was followed by a massacre, the town was looted, and the inhabitants that escaped sought refuge on Zakynthos.

For years there was a "tower" near the harbour, consisting of the skulls and bones of the Venetian and Greek defenders of the fortress massacred by Bayezid II: *"They say that from the great slaughter they made, the blood ran into the sea and turned it red ... And he ordered all the Methonians captured alive to be brought before him, young and old. And he ordered that all those over 10 years should be cut down, and so it was done. And they gathered their heads and bodies and built and made a large tower outside the castle."* (K. Simopoulos, *Ξένοι ταξιδιώτες στην Ελλάδα*, I, Athens 1972, p. 362)

In 1531, the Knights of Saint John, who had been expelled from Rhodes, attacked Methone and succeeded in capturing the fortress. They abandoned it, however, taking 1,600 prisoners with them, for fear of a fierce counter-attack from the Turks.

In 1572, the victors of the battle of Lepanto, led by Don John of Austria, made an unsuccessful attempt to capture Methone.

Methone, now only sparsely inhabited but still an important trading post, passed into the hands of Venice once more in 1685 after a siege of the fortress lasting three weeks. The incessant cannon bombardment during this siege is said to have reduced the women and children to a state of hysteria in which they screamed so much that the men shut them up in the Bourtzi.

During the thirty years that they held the Peloponnese, the Venetians governed harshly and oppressively. In addition to his mili-

Fig. 164. Fortress of Methone. Ibrahim's residence. Maison established himself here, and the Venetian provveditori probably also lived here until 1500 and between 1685 and 1715.

Fig. 165. Fortress of Methone. The south side of the small enclosure, which housed the residences of whoever was master of the fortress at the time. In front of the wall was the road to the market, which ended at the west at the pyramidal gunpowder magazine.
The monolithic granite column (height 3.67 m.) that can be seen is probably from the "shipwreck of the columns" at Sapienza (see fig. 174-175).

Fig. 166. Fortress of Methone. The paved road directly inside the main gate, from the north. The road led to the complex of the two arched gates, and from there to the large enclosure.

Fig. 167. Fortress of Methone. The same road from the south.

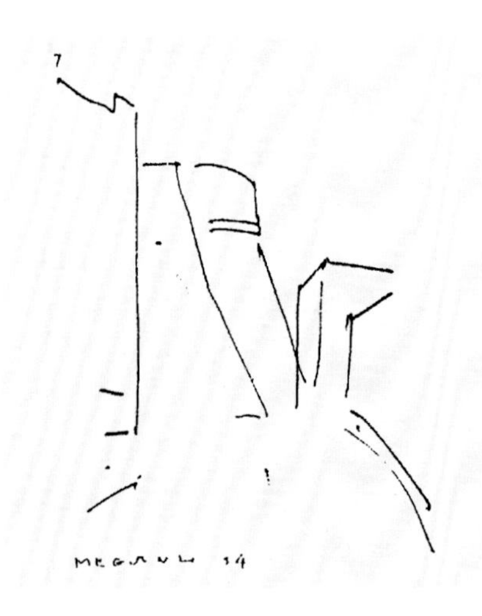

Fig. 168. Fortress of Methone. The imposing arched bridge over the moat and the gate at the north entrance to the fortress, which were repaired by the engineers of the French expeditionary corps.

tary responsibilities, the garrison commander *(castellano)* was also in charge of applying strict market regulations. Inhabitants of Methone who were not Venetians were not allowed to sell, rent, or mortgage without special permission: in other words, they had no right to exploit their property which, by definition, belonged to Venice, not themselves.

Venetian engineers repaired, rebuilt, and constructed major extensions and additions to the defences of the fortress. The settlement inside the fortress had narrow streets and densely built houses, mainly of timber.

The west side of the enclosure, with its five plain rectangular towers, possibly dates from the early Venetian period. The wild, rocky shores and strong winds made it impossible for ships to draw close to this part of the fortress.

The major projects constructed during the Second Venetian period include the Loredan bastion and the realignment of the moat, and the defence works at the west end of the moat. The moat was never filled with seawater and the work of deepening it was never completed. There is evidence, in the form of inscriptions at Methone and official reports by Venetian governors, confirming that building work on the Methone fortress continued until 1714, one year before the Turks returned and finally expelled the Venetians.

After the recapture of Methone by the Turks, its population increased, as did traffic in the harbour. This attracted the interest of the French, who founded a consulate here in 1747, after French commercial establishments dealing in agricultural products had already established themselves in the town.

The Belgian De Mirone, who visited the area in 1719, described Methone as the finest harbour in the Peloponnese.

Before the Greek War of Independence of 1821, Methone had 4,500 Turkish inhabitants, and was never captured by the Greek freedom fighters, despite their incessant attacks. Ibrahim was thus

Fig. 169. Fortress of Methone. The south wall of the small enclosure with the area of the large enclosure behind it. The church of 1828 can be seen, and also the base of the minaret, the tall building to the east, the inside of the complex of towers at the south gate, and behind this the Bourtzi, with the island of Sapienza in the distance.

Fig. 170. Fortress of Methone. South-west end, where the mode of construction used in the outer fortification wall can be seen at a point that has collapsed.

able to find a secure harbour for his fleet in 1825. Ibrahim and his General Staff established themselves at Methone, which became an Egyptian base of operations during his campaign in the Peloponnese. Maison entered the fortress of Methone in November 1828 after negotiations, without having to offer battle. After the withdrawal of the Egyptians, the new town was built outside the fortress, under the guidance of the French engineers. The town plan of Methone, like that of Pylos, is the work of the French.

The educational policy pursued by the first prime-minister of the newly independent Greek state, Ioannis Kapodistrias, involved the foundation of schools, one of which still survives at Methone.

Methone was for millennia a port of call on the sea route around the Peloponnese. Its natural harbour, sheltered from the north wind, and the islet of Sapienza opposite were also a refuge for ships that put in here to seek protection from adverse weather conditions. Tes-

Fig. 171. Fortress of Methone. The south-east end of the fortress with the Bourtzi in the distance.

Fig. 172. Fortress of Methone. The Bembo bastion in the north-east part of the fortress, with the moat and earthwork in front of it.

Fig. 173. Letter written by Ioannis Kapodistrias to the French consul Theophile Feburier in June 1831. The prime minister refers to the foundation of the Model and Central School on Aigina (1829).

The Kapodistrias school at Methone.

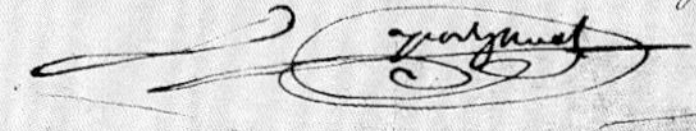

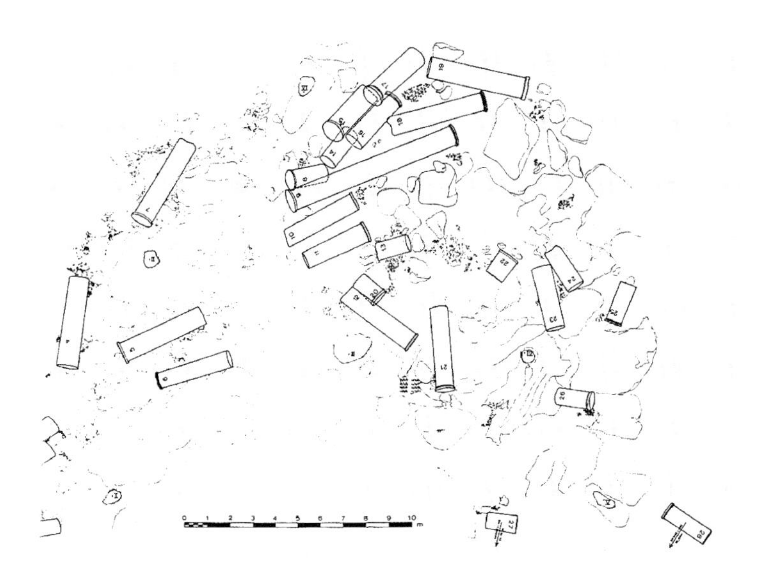

Fig. 174-175. Island of Sapienza. Cape Spitha. Measured drawing and underwater photograph of the "shipwreck of the columns".

timony to this role played by Methone is furnished by the layer of pottery of all periods at the bottom of the bay of Methone, and the well-known shipwrecks located along the north coast of Sapienza: the "wreck of the columns", dating from the 4th c. AD, near cape Spitha on the island, which had a cargo of columns made of Egyptian granite, the "wreck of the sarcophagi", dating from the 2nd or 3rd c. AD, and the wreck of a British warship that went down in the 19th c.

Nothing has survived of the settlement and buildings inside the fortress, other than a Turkish bathhouse, the remains of the minaret at the south-west corner of the church of Saint Ioannis, the small pyramidal building (gunpowder magazine), and a large number of water cisterns.

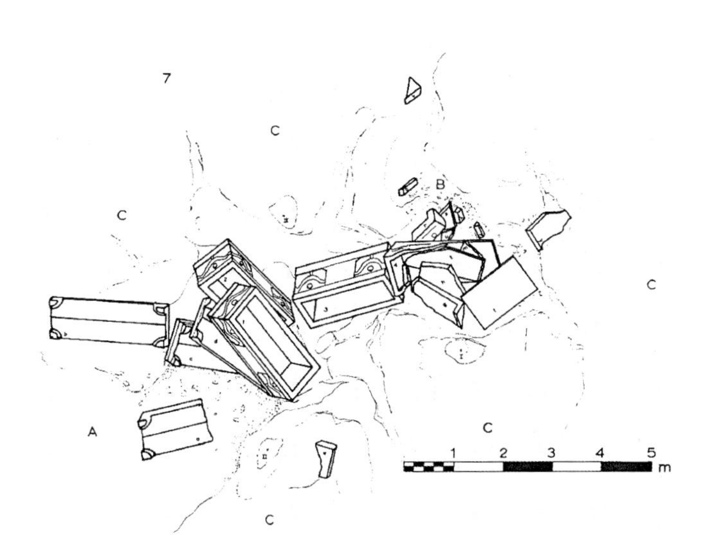

Fig. 176-177. Island of Sapienza. Cape Spitha. Measured drawing and underwater photograph of the "shipwreck of the sarcophagi". The sarcophagi were made of Egyptian granite and decorated with relief bucrania and garlands.

Fig. 178. Bronze figurine of a hoplite found in the sanctuary of Apollo Korythos to the south of temple Γ. National Archaeological Museum, Athens.

CORONE

Three ancient coastal cities evolved in Pylia, along the east coast of the Akritas peninsula. These were the small town of Kolonides, probably near Ayios Andreas, to which probably belonged the nearby sanctuary of Apollo Korythos at Longa dating from the Geometric period; ancient Corone, founded in 369 BC at modern Petalidi, where building remains of the ancient city have been identified; and Asine, a city attested from the 5th c. BC onwards, on the site of modern Corone.

Excavations conducted in 1915 by the archaeologist Fr. Versakis at Longa, 14 km. south of Petalidi, yielded evidence for the religious worship going back to the early Geometric period, possibly as early as the 10th c. BC. Temples and buildings ranging in date from the Archaic to the Hellenistic period were uncovered on this site, as well as a large number of offerings dedicated to the worship of Apollo Korythos. The sanctuary includes five temples (A, B, Γ, Δ, E), the earliest of which are B, Δ, and E. Temple B, of the 8th c. BC, was built of stone and clay, had three bays, a wooden entablature faced with clay, and a tiled roof. Temple E, a Doric peripteral temple of the 7th c. BC, is a broad, spacious structure with two bays. The large Doric peripteral temple Γ is later in date, of the 6th c. BC, and has an unusual colonnade and a double cella *in antis*, which, at a much later date, formed the central aisle of a Christian three-aisled basilica. Temple A, an Ionic building, was erected in the 4th c. BC after the destruction of temple Γ. The architectural remains of this monument, which was seen intact by Pausanias, attest to successive building phases down to the end of the Roman empire.

The epithet "Korythos" applied to Apollo possibly derives from the noun korys (genitive: korythos), which means summit, or crested helmet, and denotes the god's military capacity. Apollo Korythos,

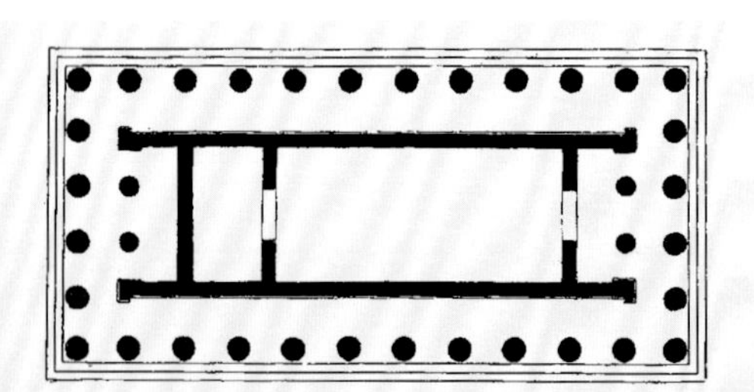

Fig. 179. Sanctuary of Apollo Korythos. Reconstruction drawing of the plan of temple Γ after Fr. Versakis.

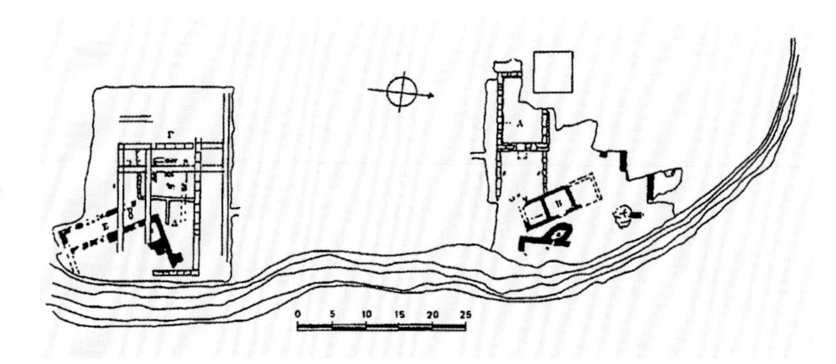

Fig. 180. Sanctuary of Apollo Korythos. Plan.

however, was also a healing deity, as Pausanias tells us (IV, 34, 7). This is apparent, too, from the design of temple E, inside which there were couches, suggesting that it functioned as an Asklepieion. A similar cult of Apollo in the double aspect of military and healing god is found at Bassai in Arkadia, where Apollo was worshipped as Epikourios, and at Sparta, where there was a cult of Apollo Amyklaios.

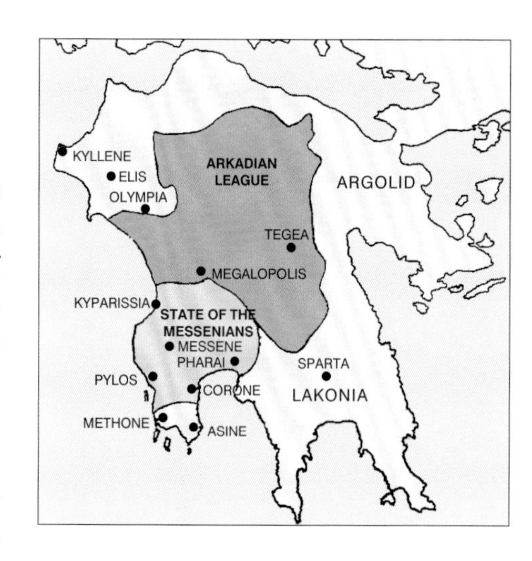

Fig. 181. The states of the Messenians and Arkadians formed after the victories of Epaminondas over the Spartans.

In the early decades of the 4th c. BC, Thebes emerged as the most powerful political and military power amongst the Greek cities. Under the leadership of Epaminondas, the Boeotians for a time ruled Akarnania and Euboea and extended their influence to Thessaly and Macedonia. Through their campaigns in the Peloponnese they crushed the Spartans and dismembered the Spartan state. Epaminondas sought through his victorious campaigns to keep Sparta under control by offering support to its traditional enemies: the Arkadians to the north and the Messenians to the west. To this end he founded Megalopolis as capital of the Arkadian League, and Messene, as capital of the Messenians. It was at this time, in 369 BC, that Corone was founded by Epimelides, a Boeotian from Coroneia, on the site now occupied by Petalidi, a few kilometres north of modern Corone.

During the Roman empire, the traveller Pausanias visited Corone, and informs us that a bronze statue of Athena stood in the open on the acropolis, and that there was a bronze statue of Zeus Soter in the agora. In the city were temples of Artemis Paidotrophos, Dionysos, and Asklepios, and the tomb of the founder, Epimelides. Traces of the ancient jetty in the harbour, now under the sea, can be seen at Petalidi, along with the remains of buildings dating from Roman times, but there are no visible remains of the ancient fortification walls and buildings mentioned by Pausanias. Corone seems to have been the seat of a Christian bishopric in the 4th c. AD.

During the Byzantine period, Corone was abandoned in the 9th c. and the inhabitants settled further south at another ancient city, Asine, on the site of the modern town of Corone.

Fig. 182. Petalidi. Ancient Corone. Bathhouse (?) of Roman date.

At the highest point of modern Corone, directly above the remains of the temple of Apollo, stand the ruins of an Early Christian basilica, built in contact with the domed cross-vaulted Byzantine church of Saint Sophia. Here, too, is the convent of the followers of the old calendar, dedicated to Saint John, which is still a functioning institution. The group of historical monuments continues to the east with the 17th c. church of Saint Charalambos, which has a campanile built on the base of a demolished minaret at the north-west corner, and an old cemetery which is still in use.

According to a Latin inscription of 1689 in the gynaikonitis, the church of Saint Charalambos was originally dedicated to the Catholic saint Rocco, who protected people against epidemics:

Fig. 183. Fortress of Corone. The Byzantine church of Saint Sophia built on the ruins of the temple of Apollo and the Early Christian basilica. In the right background can be seen the church of Saint Charalambos.

MDCDLXXXIX / DIVO ROCHO / OB URBEM A PESTE LIBERATAM / MILITIAE VOTUM / MDCLXXXXVIII ADEMPTUM

The church of San Rocco was converted into a mosque and a minaret added to it; after 1829 it became a Christian church once more, dedicated to Saint Charalambos.

These monuments form a fine architectural complex of sacred buildings of all periods and religious creeds and persuasions, testifying to the continuity of religion and promoting the beliefs held at various times.

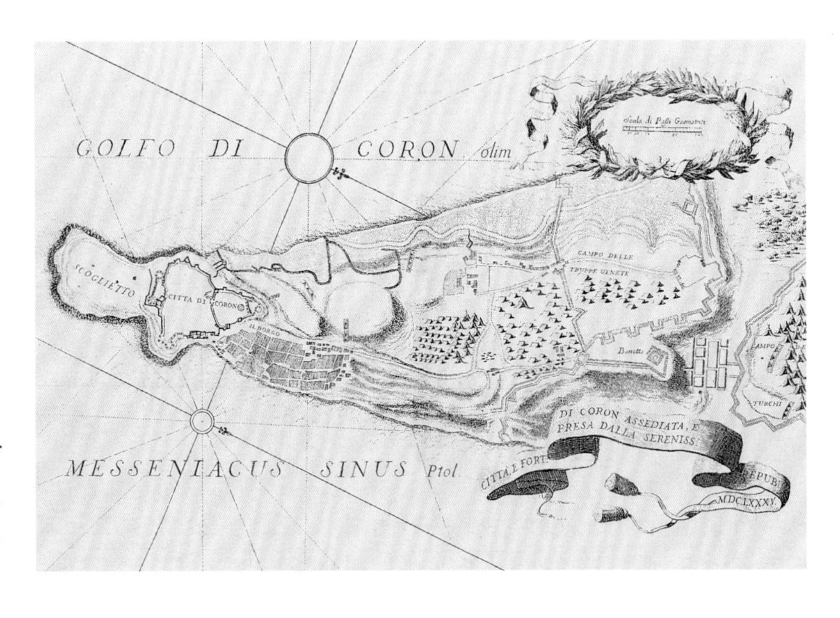

Fig. 184. Corone. The Venetian siege of the fortress. Drawing by Coronelli who accompanied Morosini and described and illustrated the military events of the campaign.

Fig. 185. Fortress of Corone. The two stout round bastions at the north-east corner of the fortress, protecting the entrance to the harbour.

In 1205 Corone was captured by the Franks and ceded to Geoffrey Villhardouin, but the Venetians expelled the Frankish garrison in 1207 and occupied the town. Corone was then strengthened with extensive defence works and, together with Methone, became a port of call for Venetian ships and secured Venetian trade with the Orient. In 1209 the Venetians, who had occupied south Messenia and enjoyed exclusive use of the harbours here, obliged the Franks to conclude a peace treaty that confined them to the Principate of Achaia.

Fig. 186. Corone. The flat promontory to the east of the fortress which was controlled by the strong bastions at the moat.

Fig. 187. Fortress of Corone. Slab with coats-of-arms and an inscription recording Venetian repairs to the fortress in 1690.

Corone, now under Venetian control and a vital link in the commercial activities of the West European mercantile powers, emerged as an important trade centre of international repute and with a highly developed economy.

Drawing mainly on information from Venetian documents, Freddy Thiriet, who has researched the archives of Venice, writes that no one could have imagined that the agricultural output of the limited territory of Corone and Methone – which was particularly fertile between Pylos and Methone – would have been of such great importance to the Venetians.

In 1500, after besieging and capturing Methone, the Turks laid siege to Corone. The residents in the castle, aware of the massacre at Methone, expressed their opposition to the Venetian garrison, which was prepared to offer resistance, and abandoned the city, having first agreed with the Turks that they should be taken to Kephalonia. The Turks in this way made themselves masters of Corone, which they held until 1532, when the famous harbour became the theatre of fresh military operations. This was the period of the rein of Suleiman the Magnificent (1494-1556) and the major expansion of the Ottoman Turks, who even laid siege to the Habsburg capital, Vienna (1529).

In 1532, the Genoese admiral Andrea Doria, at the head of a powerful naval force of about 90 Genoese, Spanish, Papal, and Maltese ships, occupied Patra, Corone, and Tunis for Charles V. Doria managed to capture Corone after his third assault from the small, unfortified headland at the east end of the fortress, and established a garrison of 8,000 men in it. The Turks returned a few months later, however, and placed the castle under an asphyxiating siege. In 1534 the Christian defenders agreed to abandon it and depart to southern Italy. These events had no effect on the amount of traffic in the port, which was undimin-

Fig. 188. Fortress of Corone. The successive defence lines on the east side of the fortress can clearly be made out. At the end of the moat are the ruins of the round bastion blown up by the Germans in 1944. The fortification walls above the moat also served as retaining walls for earth deposits.

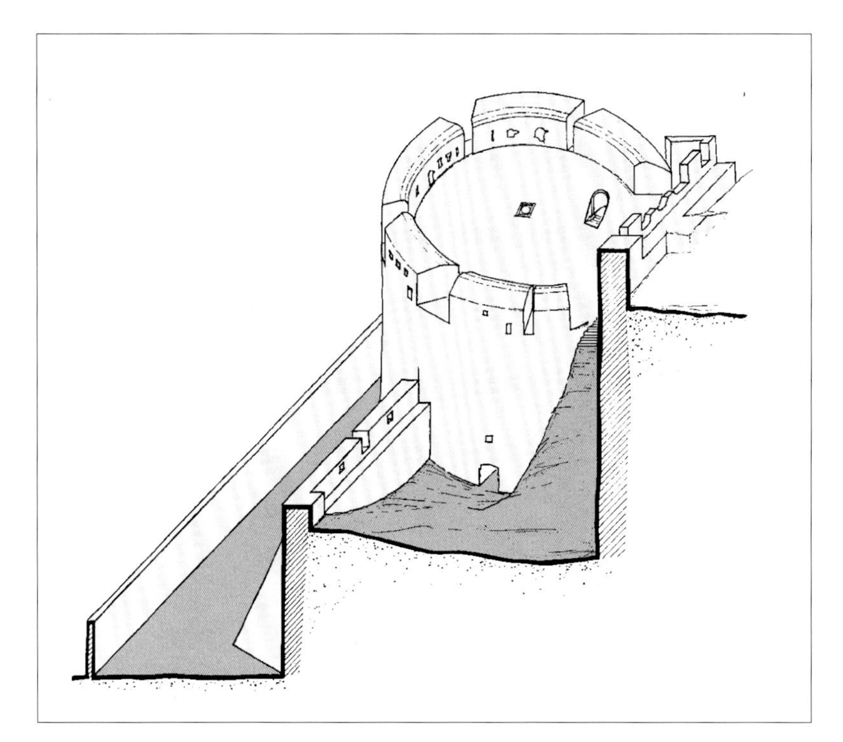

Fig. 189. Fortress of Corone. The successive defence lines on the east side, with the round bastion.

ished; the new rulers, the Turks, engaged in strong trading activity in the 16th and 17th c., mainly exporting olive-oil, wool and silk.

In 1685, Doge Francesco Morosini initiated his campaign to recapture the Peloponnese at Corone. Morosini besieged Corone, captured the area to the west of the fortress and created a defence line stretching from the north to the south coast, thereby preventing reinforcements from Kalamata from reaching the besieged Turks. His concerted lightning attack on all sides of the castle, combined with the undermining and blowing up of the west bastion, obliged the Turks to surrender, and the Venetians returned to Corone after an absence of about two centuries. The report sent by the general *provveditore* of the Peloponnese, Corner, to the *Serenissima Repubblica*, is indicative:

"There then follows the camp of Corone, which is not without its virtues. It stands at the end of a promontory, equipped with towers after the old custom, and is the capital of a large, fertile region. The Holy council knows the damage suffered during the siege, which I did not fail to restore. I fixed the Maltese breach and repaired the parts near the large breach which were most likely to collapse, as has been made clear to your Excellencies by the reports and drawings I respectfully submitted to you. If we could finish the works I have ordered to seal the breach and unify the fortifications, we would secure ourselves well enough, which is something that any proper assessment vigorously recommends."

(*Πελοποννησιακά* 15 (1982-84), p. 144)

During the Second Venetian period Corone is said to have been famous for craftsmen who produced siege engines. This item of information calls to mind the Spartans during the Peloponnesian War: wishing

Fig. 190. "Corone pithoi" in a pottery workshop that functioned at Vounaria in Pylia until 1972.

to neutralise the pocket of Athenians in Koryphasion, they sent ships to Asine (Byzantine Corone), to fetch timber for their siege machines, since they estimated that this was the only way in which they would be able to capture the high wall built by Demosthenes overlooking the harbour (Thucydides IV, 13).

In the Turkish period, the fortress of Corone was one of the strongest defence works in the Peloponnese, and undoubtedly the strongest in Messenia. The fortification architecture can be seen in the structures intended to reinforce its defence capability: high towers-bastions, cannon on the walls in a succession of defence lines; it can also be discerned in the way the vertical natural rock-faces were consolidated and covered with built, protective "stone cloaks".

There was no natural source of water in the fortress of Corone, a feature it shared with those of Navarino and Methone. A supply of water was secured by means of aqueducts and a great number of cisterns, each with a large capacity.

The British officer W. Leake, who visited Corone in the early years of the 19th c., gives the following account of what he saw: *"... there are 200 Turkish families in the fortress, and 130 Greek in the suburb... The Greek Varusi as well as the Turkish town in the castle is built of sun-baked bricks; the Turkish houses are in a state of ruin and desolation, but the fortress itself is in better repair and of a better construction than those of Neokastro and Mothoni... In good years the export of oil from Koroni amounts to 15,000 barrels; but here, as elsewhere, the alternate crops of oil are generally deficient... The only other commodity exported from Koroni is the silk already mentioned."*

(W.M. Leake, *Travels in the Morea*, 1, London 1830, p. 436-438)

Another traditional activity pursued by the inhabitants of the region is the production of the well-known Corone pithoi.

Livadia, a small tongue of land on the east side of the fortress, is controlled by a strong fortification complex involving successive lines

Fig. 191. Fortress of Corone. The tall round south bastion over the moat on the east side of the fortress.

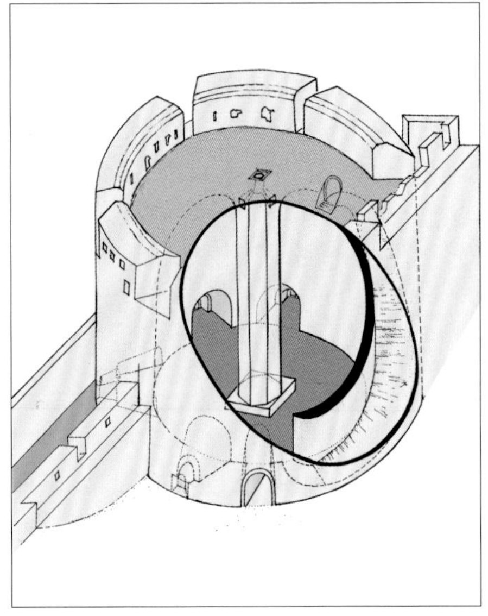

Fig. 192. Fortress of Corone. The round south bastion on the east side.

Fig. 193. Fortress of Corone. The octagonal pillar in the south bastion.

of defence. This complex consists of a thin outer wall 2 m. high, built on the east edge of a deep moat 15 m. wide, the west edge of which is protected by a fortification wall rising 13 m. above the bottom of the moat, and by two round tower-like bastions at the ends of this fortification wall. The northern of these two bastions was demolished by the retreating Germans in 1944, who ignited the munitions they had stored in it.

The southern bastion on the moat has a characteristic huge octagonal pillar at the centre with a side of 0.40 m., diameter of 2.20 m., and height of 11 m. This pillar rises to the roof vault and supports the flat roof with its five cannon emplacements. There are four cannon embrasures in the bastion, the two outer ones being sealed up. The cannon embrasures and the entrance are bounded by elaborate arched structures. The staircase-ramp of circular plan that leads up to the flat roof of the tower is built in the thickness of the wall. In an attempt to date the structures, Kevin Andrews writes of the impressive defence works on the east side of the fortress (*Castles of the Morea*, 1953, p. 20): *"This complex of fortifications on the castle's east flank resembles in size the monumental works of the Venetians, but the style of construction and the materials, particularly the tiles, are more closely related to the Turkish fortifications of the XVI century. After the battle of Lepanto in 1571 and the raids of Don John along the Messenian coast, the Turks were busy adding to the defences of Methone and building a new castle at Navarino. Corone, the strongest citadel of all, would hardly have been neglected."*

During the Greek Uprising of 1821, the Greeks besieged the fortress but failed to take it. The forts of Corone and Methone were surrendered by the Turks to the French general Maison in 1828.

Like all the castles in the Peloponnese, Niokastro at Pylos and the forts of Methone and Corone enclosed and protected settlements that had quite well-designed street networks. Of all the fortresses in Messenia, it is only at Corone that life can still be found in the settlement within the walls, alongside the traditional settlement outside the walls.

Fig. 194. Corone. Monument in honour of the 50 Coronians massacred by the Turks after they entered the fortress during the final, unsuccessful Greek assault on 28 February 1824. The site of the battle is still called Resalto (Onslaught).

Fig. 195. Corone. The approach to the main entrance of the fortress, created by the French engineers of general Maison.

Postscript

In fact it is impossible to do justice to this complex phenomenon by rigid classification. Transhumance implies all sorts of conditions, physical, human and historical. In the Mediterranean, in its simplest form, it is a vertical movement from the winter pastures of the plain to the summer pastures in the hills. It is a way of life combining the two levels, and at the same time a source of human migration. These men may belong to one village or another, one rural – or non-rural – group or another; they may be simple shepherds, or they may, during one of their stays, hastily cultivate the earth, sometimes burning the scrubland in autumn to make crops grow more quickly; they may have their homes in the hills or on the plains; they

may or may not have fixed dwellings. In short there are many variations on the theme, but they are imposed by local conditions and are virtually unavoidable. One anecdote deserves mention. Coron, on the Greek coast, was in 1499 still a Venetian outpost. The Pasha of Morea wanted to prevent the Albanians and Greeks of the little town from sowing crops or grazing flocks on the territory of the Grand Turk. The Rettori of Coron merely replied dolcemente, "Our flocks may go to your land in summer, but your flocks come to ours in winter."

(F. Braudel, *The Mediterranean*, 1995, p. 87)

Fig. 196. Fortress of Korone. The east side of the defence works with the flat tongue of land in front of them.

TERMINOLOGY OF FORTRESS ARCHITECTURE

battlement: a parapet with open spaces, built on top of a castle wall, tower or fort.
chemin de ronde: narrow communicating corridor on the battlement of a castle.
citadel: a fortress on a commanding height defending a city.
curtain wall: the wall between two bastions or towers.
embrasure: an opening with the sides slanted so that it is wider on the outside than on the inside.
glacis: gently sloping embankment as part of defensive system.
gorgyra: interior vaulted room of a bastion.
moat: a deep wide ditch dug around a fortress or castle, often filled with water.
outwork: a lesser trench or fortification built outside the main defences.
passageway: wide corridor on the battlements of a castle, housing cannons.
portcullis: a heavy iron grating suspended by chains and lowered between grooves to bar the gateway of a castle.
rampart: an embankment of earth surmounted by a parapet encircling a castle.

CHRONOLOGICAL TABLE

5300-3200 BC Neolithic settlements at Koryphasion, Voidokilia, Prophitis Ilias, and sites in the area around the bay of Pylos.

3200-2000/1900 BC Important Early Helladic installation at Voidokilia.

19th-16th c. BC Traces of Middle Helladic settlement at Voidokilia. Minyan ware pottery.

16th-13th c. BC Zenith of the Mycenaean kingdom at Pylos. Large Mycenaean Palace of Neleus and Palace of Nestor, at Epano Englianos. Mycenaean settlements and installations and tholos and chamber tombs densely distributed over the whole of Messenia. The bay of Pylos was the harbour of the Neleid state. The so-called Tomb of Thrasymedes at Voidokilia built on the remains of Early Helladic settlement and a Middle Helladic tumulus.

13th c. BC Use of Linear B script in Greece.

1250 BC Capture of Troy. Transitional period from the Late Helladic IIIB to IIIC pottery style.

1200 BC Palace of Nestor destroyed by fire. Abandonment of Epano Englianos.

Before 1000 BC Greeks (Ionians and Aeolians) colonise the west coast of Asia Minor.

9th-8th c. BC Homeric poems.

776 BC Beginning of records of Olympic victors.

743-724 BC First Messenian War. Messenians subjected by Spartans.

685-667 BC Second Messenian War. Revolt of the Messenian helots. The Spartans prove victorious and the Pylians, with the Methonians and other Messenians, flee and settle at Zankle in Sicily, to which they give the name Messene. The Spartans bring in settlers from Nauplion.

464-454 BC Third Messenian War. General revolt of the Messenian helots develops into a fierce war against Sparta and ends in the comprehensive defeat of the insurgents.

431 BC Athenians attempt unsuccessfully to detach Methone from the Spartans.

425 BC During the course of the Peloponnesian War the Athenian general Demosthenes fortifies Koryphasion and establishes a garrison there. Clash between the Athenians and Spartans at Koryphasion and Sphakteria. Defeat of Spartans, who are taken prisoner.

413 BC Athenian garrison at Pylos engages in raids on Messenia, which they pillage and desolate.

410-409 BC Syracusan general Hermokrates assists the Spartans in their operations against Pylos. Pylos surrenders to the Spartans.

369 BC Independent Messenian state founded with its capital at Messene, after the campaign of Epaminondas in the Peloponnese and the defeat of the Spartans at Mantineia.

337 BC Congress of the Greeks at Corinth called by Philip II, king of Macedonia. Decision taken to wage war on Persia.

334 BC Alexander the Great crosses the Hellespont. Start of a ten-year campaign that destroys the Persian empire.

331 BC Foundation of Alexandria in Egypt. Pylos becomes a member of the Achaian Confederacy.

146 BC-4th c. AD Roman rule in Greece. Achaian Confederacy dissolved and Pylos returned to the Messenians.

31 BC Battle of Actium. Antony and Cleopatra defeated by Octavian.

AD 176 Pausanias visits Messenia.

AD 193-211 During the reign of Severus coins are struck at Pylos bearing the word ΠΥΛΙΩΝ ("of the Pylians") on the reverse.

330 Constantinople becomes the capital of the Roman empire after the imperial edict issued by Constantine the Great.

393 Last Olympic games.

533 Justinian's general Belisarius at Methone.

1071 Battle of Manzikert. Terrible defeat inflicted on the Byzantine forces under the emperor Romanos IV Diogenes by the sultan Arp-Arslan.

1125 Methone destroyed and desolated by the Venetians.

1153 The Arab cosmographer Edresi writes that Methone is fortified.

1204 Fourth Crusade. Franks and Venetians capture and loot Constantinople. Byzantine empire dismembered and conquerors share out Greek territories. Geoffrey Villhardouin occupies Methone.

1206 Venetian fleet captures Methone and Corone.

1261 Greeks expel the Franks and recover the throne of Constantinople. Emperor Michael VIII Palaiologos (1261-1282).

1278 Castle of Navarino (Paliokastro) built at Koryphasion by the Frankish ruler of Thebes, Nikolaos II of the Saint Omer family.

1318 Paliokastro captured by the Genoese.

1366 Paliokastro reverts to the Franks of Marie of Bourbonne.

1381 Spanish mercenaries from Navarre settle on the bay.

1453 Turks capture Constantinople. End of the Byzantine empire.

1479 Peace treaty between Venice and the Turks. Venice holds Naupaktos, Methone, Monemvasia and Navarino.

1498 Portuguese explorer Vasco da Gama discovers the sea route to India by circumnavigating Africa. Commercial activity ceases to be the prerogative of Mediterranean powers and is centred in the hands of countries washed by the Atlantic ocean. This, together with the Turkish capture of Egypt and – from 1500 – of Methone and Corone, the traditional Venetian bases on the maritime commercial routes, marked the beginning of the end for the Venetian empire.

1499-1500 Sultan Bayezid II captures Corone, Methone and Paliokastro.

1501 Paliokastro captured by Demetrios, a Greek in the service of the Venetian garrison at Methone, at the head of 50 Greeks, mostly volunteers from Crete and the Ionian islands. Shortly afterwards, the Greek garrison and its leader are attacked and annihilated by the Turks under the pirate Kemal.

1529 First unsuccessful siege of Vienna by the Turks.

1571 Battle of Lepanto (Naupaktos). Turkish fleet destroyed by the combined fleet of Venice, Spain and Pope Pius V, under Don John of Austria.

1572 Unsuccessful attempts by Don John to capture Paliokastro and Methone. To protect the bay of Navarino, the base of operations for their fleet, the Turks block the northern strait with earth deposits to prevent the large enemy vessels from entering.

1573 The Turks complete the protection and reinforcement of the bay of Navarino by building a new fortress, Niokastro, at the southern entrance to the bay, controlling the Great Passage.

1683 Second unsuccessful siege of Vienna by the Turks.

1684-1687 Morosini and the Swedish general Königsmark capture all the castles on the coast of the Peloponnese held by Turks.

1715 All the fortresses in the Morea recaptured by the Turks. End of the period known as the Second Venetian period in the Morea (1685-1715).

1770 The Orloff episode. As part of the operations of the Russo-Turkish war, the Russian brothers Alexandros and Theodoros Orloff land at Oitylo and attempt to rouse the Greeks to revolt. They fail to take Methone and Corone but make themselves masters of the bay of Navarino and Niokastro after a siege lasting six days. The Turkish garrison of Niokastro surrenders and is massacred. After the departure of the Russians, the Turks recapture Niokastro with the aid of Albanians. Remorseless, unprecedented massacre of the Greek population. Many of the inhabitants of the Peloponnese flee to Asia Minor.

1821 Greek War of Independence begins. Niokastro captured by the Greeks under Yiorgos Ikonomidis and Grigorios bishop of Methone. Fortresses of Methone and Corone besieged but not captured.

1825

11 February: Ibrahim's first landing at Methone.

14 March: Ibrahim attacks Niokastro.

15 March: Battle at Schinolakkas. Greek victory.

7 April: Battle at Kremmydia. Greek defeat.

26 April: Ibrahim captures Sphakteria. Anagnostakis, Tsamados, Santa Rosa, and many other freedom fighters killed during the fighting. The brig *Ares* heroically forces its way through the blockade by the Turkish-Egyptian fleet at the bay of Navarino.

30 April: Paliokastro surrenders to Ibrahim. One of Ibrahim's squadrons destroyed by Miaoulis in the bay of Methone.

11 May: Ibrahim captures Niokastro.

20 May: Battle against Ibrahim at Maniaki. Heroic deaths of Papaphlessas and a further 200 Greek insurgents.

1825-1827 Ibrahim master of the Peloponnese.

1827 (20 October) Battle of Navarino. The allied fleet of Britain, France and Russia, which had orders to compel Ibrahim to refrain from pillaging the Morea, defeats the Turkish and Egyptian fleet anchored in the bay.

1828

January: Death of Alexandros Ypsilandis in Vienna.

February: After the capture and destruction of Tripolis, Ibrahim moves to Pylia and establishes himself in the Methone-Corone-Pylos triangle.

June: The three victorious admirals of the battle of Navarino meet off Methone and exercise pressure on Ibrahim to withdraw from the Peloponnese.

August-September: French expeditionary force of 15,000 men under general Maison lands at Petalidi (ancient Corone) to receive the surrender of the fortresses by Ibrahim.

September: Ibrahim withdraws from the Peloponnese with the last of the Egyptian army. The French engineers begin to build the towns of Pylos and Methone, outside the walls of the fortresses. The settlements inside the walls are demolished to provide building material for the new towns.

1829 General Maison and the larger part of the French expeditionary force leave the Peloponnese.

1834 Niokastro converted into a prison for long-term convicts, for about a century.

1939 Archaeologists C.W. Blegen and K. Kourouniotis locate the Palace of Nestor at Epano Englianos and dig the first trial trenches.

1941-1943 Under the Italian-German Occupation during the Second World War, Niokastro is made a headquarters of the Italian forces. In 1943-1944, after the Italian capitulation, it became a German headquarters.

1941 Italian ship *Sebastiano Veniero* torpedoed to the west of Methone, with the loss of the British prisoners-of-war it was transporting. A cemetery is created for them in the fortress of Methone.

1952-1968 Excavations in the Palace of Nestor.

1952 Systematic excavation of the Palace of Nestor begun by C.W. Blegen of the University of Cincinnati. M. Ventris deciphers Linear B. Sp. Marinatos excavates the Mycenaean cemetery at Volimidia, Chora.

1958-1960 René Puaux collection and finds from the excavation of the Mycenaean tombs at Koukounara by Sp. Marinatos placed on exhibition by G. Papathanassopoulos in the Antonopouleion Museum in Pylos. Exhibition of finds from the Palace of Nestor in the Chora Museum by N. Yialouris.

1964-1969 Excavation of the Hellenistic tumulus at Tsopani Rachi and exhibition of the finds in the Pylos Museum by G. Papathanassopoulos.

1982-1986 Extensive consolidation and restoration work at Niokastro as preparation for the foundation and functioning of the Pylos Centre of Underwater Archaeology. Completion of the consolidation, restoration and renovation work on the two-storey Maison Barracks building, to convert it into a hostel, a library, and an exhibition room for the collection of the philhellene René Puaux, who donated his collection to the Municipality of Pylos.

1992 Part of the René Puaux collection that had been kept in the Fondation Hellénique in Paris (155 engravings, lithographs and documents) brought to Greece by G. Papathanasso-poulos, under the responsibility of Professor K. Georgoulis, the head of the Foundation.

1993 The René Puaux collection displayed in the Navarino Museum by the Ephorate of Underwater Archaeology.

ABBREVIATIONS

AAA: Athens Annals of Archaeology.
ADelt: Αρχαιολογικόν Δελτίον.
AEphem: Αρχαιολογική Εφημερίς.
AJA: American Journal of Archaeology.
Αναστήλωση, Προστασία: Αναστήλωση, Συντήρηση, Προστασία Μνημείων και Συνόλων. Τεχνική περιοδική έκδοση Υπουργείου Πολιτισμού.
BCH: Bulletin de correspondance hellénique.
BSA: The Annual of the British School of Athens.
ΔΙΕΕ: Δελτίον Ιστορικής και Εθνολογικής Εταιρείας.
EpistEpetAth: Επιστημονική Επετηρίς Φιλοσοφικής Σχολής Πανεπιστημίου Αθηνών.
EpistEpetPolytThess: Επιστημονική Επετηρίς Πολυτεχνικής Σχολής Αριστοτελείου Πανεπιστημίου Θεσσαλονίκης.
ESM: Expédition Scientifique de Morée, ordonnée par le gouvernement français. Architecture, I, Paris 1831-38.
IEE: Ιστορία του Ελληνικού Έθνους, Ekdotike Athenon.
JHS: Journal of Hellenic Studies.
PN I (1): Carl W. Blegen - Marion Rawson, *The Palace of Nestor at Pylos in Western Messenia,* I (The Buildings and their Contents), part 1 (text), Princeton 1966.
PN I (2): Carl W. Blegen - Marion Rawson, *The Palace of Nestor at Pylos in Western Messenia,* I (The Buildings and their Contents), part 2 (plates), Princeton 1966.
PN II: Mabel L. Lang, *The Palace of Nestor at Pylos in Western Messenia,* II (The Frescoes), Princeton 1969.
PN III: Carl W. Blegen - Marion Rawson - Lord William Taylor - William P. Donovan, *The Palace of Nestor at Pylos in Western Messenia,* III (Acropolis and Lower Town), Princeton 1973.
Prakt: Πρακτικά της εν Αθήναις Αρχαιολογικής Εταιρείας.

GENERAL BIBLIOGRAPHY

For the topography, mythology, history and archaeology of ancient Messenia, see N. Papachatzis, *Παυσανίου Ελλάδος περιήγησις, Μεσσηνιακά*, Athens 1979.
For the history of all periods, see *IEE*, especially the chapters: Ο Πελοποννησιακός πόλεμος, by Ch. Pelekidis (III, p. 211-214); Η λατινοκρατούμενη Ελλάδα - βενετικές και γενουατικές κτήσεις, by Ch. Maltezou (IX, p. 244-278); *eadem*, Το Δεσποτάτο του Μορέως (1262-1461) (IX, p. 282-291). For the period 1821-1829, see op.cit., XII (Η Ελληνική Επανάσταση), the work of D. Photiadis, *Η Επανάσταση του Εικοσιένα*, Athens 1971 and G. Finley, *History of the Greek Revolution*, Edinburgh - London MDCCCLXI.
For the testimony of foreign travellers, see K. Simopoulos, *Ξένοι ταξιδιώτες στην Ελλάδα, I, 333 μ.Χ.-1700,* Athens 1972, *II, 1700-1800*, Athens 1973; *idem*, *Πώς είδαν οι ξένοι την Ελλάδα του '21*, 5 (1826-1829), Athens 1984; W.M. Leake, *Travels in the Morea*, 1, London 1830, p. 395-451, who visited Messenia in 1805.
For the history of the Mediterranean peoples in relation to their environment, see F. Braudel, *The Mediterranean*, 1995.

SUBJECT BIBLIOGRAPHY

For archaeological excavations and finds of the Neolithic, Early Helladic, Middle Helladic and Late Helladic-Mycenaean periods in the south-west Peloponnese, especially Pylos, see M.N. Valmin, *Etudes topographiques sur la Messénie ancienne*, Lund 1930. For the Palace of Nestor, see C.W. Blegen - K. Kourouniotis, Ανασκαφαί Πύλου (Εγκλιανός), *AEphem* 1939, Chronika, p. 1-16 and C.W. Blegen - K. Kourouniotis, Excavations at Pylos, *AJA* 43 (1939), p. 557-576; C.W. Blegen, The Palace of Nestor: Excavations at Pylos 1952, *AJA* 57 (1953), p. 59-64, pl. 30-37; *idem*, The Palace of Nestor: Excavations of 1954, *AJA* 59 (1955), p. 31-37, pl. 23-28; C.W. Blegen - M. Lang, The Palace of Nestor: Excavations of 1959, *AJA* 60 (1960), p. 153-164, pl. 39-48; *PN I (1-2); PN II; PN III;* C.W. Blegen, *A Guide to the Palace of Nestor*, University of Cincinnati 1967; G. Lolos, *Το ανάκτορον του Νέστορος*, 1972; M. Pandelidou, Το πρόβλημα της ομηρικής Πύλου, *AAA* II (1969), p. 309-322;

R. Hope Simpson - W.A. McDonald, Prehistoric Habitation in Southwestern Peloponnese, *AJA* 65 (1961), p. 250-251. For the seven cities offered by Agamemnon to Achilles, see R. Hope Simpson, Identifying a Mycenean State, *BSA* 52 (1957), p. 231-259, pl. 47-50; E. Vermeule, *Greece in the Bronge Age*, University of Chicago 1964; O. Dickinson, *The Origins of the Mycenaean Civilisation*, Götemborg 1977; M. Sakellariou, Ένα πρόβλημα της ομηρικής γεωγραφίας: τα όρια της χώρας των Επειών, *Πελοποννησιακά* 3-4 (1958-59), p. 17-46; S. Marinatos, Palaipylos, *Das Altertum* 1 (1955), p. 140-163; S. Marinatos, *Prakt* 1952, p. 473-496; 1953, p. 238-250; 1954, p. 299-316; 1955, p. 245-255; 1956, p. 202-206; 1957, p. 118-120; 1958, p. 184-193; 1959, p. 174-179; 1960, p. 195-209; 1961, p. 169-176; 1962, p. 90-98; 1963, p. 114-121; 1964, p. 78-95; 1965, p. 102-120; 1966, p. 119-132; see also G. Korres, *Prakt* 1975, p. 428-514, pl. 303-327; 1976, p. 253-282, pl. 172-183; 1976, p. 469-550, pl. 255-277; 1980, p. 120-187, pl. 103-130; C.W. Blegen, Ο Όμηρος, ο Στράβων και η Πύλος του Νέστορος, *EpistEpetAth* XIV (1963-64), p. 285-305. W. MacDonald - W.D.E. Coulson - J. Rosser, *Excavations at Nichoria in Southwest Greece*, Minneapolis 1983.

For Linear B, see E.L. Bennett, *The Pylos Tablets, A Preliminary Transcription*, Princeton 1951; M. Ventris - J. Chadwick, *Documents in Mycenaean Greek*, Cambridge 1956; L.R. Palmer, *The Interpretation of Mycenaean Greek Texts*, Oxford 1963; J. Chadwick, *The Decipherment of Linear B*, Cambridge 1967; J. Chadwick, Η γέννησις της ελληνικής γλώσσης, *EpistEpetAth* 12 (1961-62), p. 531-544; M. Ventris - J. Chadwick, Evidence of Greek Dialect in the Mycenaean Archives, *JHS* 73 (1953), p. 84-103; N. Masouridis, *Η μινωική γραφή εις τας πινακίδας της Πύλου*, Athens 1976; *idem*, *Αποκρυπτογράφησις της Γραμμικής Β. Μέθοδος και εφαρμογαί της*, Athens 1987; I. Probonas, *Σύντομος εισαγωγή εις την μυκηναϊκήν φιλολογίαν*, Athens 1990.

For the Tomb of Thrasymedes and Mycenaean tombs in general in the area of Pylia, see G. Korres, *Prakt* 1979, p. 138-155, pl. 105-113; Η προϊστορία της Βοϊδοκοιλιάς, *Μνήμη* 1979, p. 393-430; *Prakt* 1982, p. 191-231, pl. 129-148; Sp. Iakovidis, Περί του σχήματος των λαξευτών τάφων εις τα Βολιμίδια Μεσσηνίας, *Χαριστήριον εις Α.Κ. Ορλάνδον*, II, Athens 1966, p. 98-111; C.W. Blegen, An Early Tholos Tomb in Western Messenia, *Hesperia* 23 (1954), p. 158-162; A. Choremis, Μυκηναϊκοί και πρωτογεωμετρικοί τάφοι εις Καρποφόραν Μεσσηνίας, *AEphem* 1973, p. 25-74; K. Kilian, Η διοικητική οργάνωση της Πύλου, *Πελοποννησιακά* 15 (1982-84), p. 55-68.

For the remains of the defence works at Koryphasion and Sphakteria, and the topography of the area according to the text of Thucydides, see R.M. Burrows, Pylos and Sfacteria, *JHS* 18 (1898), p. 147-159, pl. VII-X; J.B. Wilson, *Pylos, 425 B.C.*, 1939. For a brief, comprehensive guide containing much information and a chronological chart of the history of the investigation of the Palace of Nestor and the Mycenaean remains of the area, see G. Lolos, *Πύλος Ημαθόεις*, Athens 1994; N. Yialouris, Ερμής Βούκλεψ, *AEphem* 1953-54, III, p. 162-184.

For the ancient history of Messenia, see C.A. Roebuck, *A History of Messenia from 369 to 146 B.C.*, 1941. For Sphakteria, see W.A. McDonald, Sphagia-Sfacteria, *Πελοποννησιακά* 3-4 (1958-59), p. 47-83. For the island Prote, see Pan. D. Dimakis, Η Πρώτη. Η μικρή ιστορία ενός έρημου νησιού, *Πελοποννησιακά* 15 (1982-84), p. 44-54.

For the excavations at Divari, see N. Yialouris, *ADelt* 21 (1966), Chronika, p. 164-165, pl. 158-162. For the Hellenistic tumulus at Tsopani Rachi, see G. Papathanassopoulos, *ADelt* 17 (1961-62), Chronika, p. 98, pl. 103β and 104α-γ and *ADelt* 21 (1966), Meletai, p. 184. Also see N. Kaltsas, Από τα ελληνιστικά νεκροταφεία της Πύλου, *ADelt* 38 (1938), Meletai, p. 1-77, pl. 1-40. For Ayios Onouphrios and the church of Saint Leo, see D. Pallas, Έρευνες στα μεσαιωνικά μνημεία της Μεθώνης, *ADelt* 17 (1961-62), Chronika, p. 103-105, pl. 111; G. Papathanassopoulos, *ADelt* 18 (1963), Chronika, p. 94, pl. 108στ. For the Byzantine churches of Messenia, see G. Dimitrokallis, *Βυζαντινά μνημεία Μεσσηνίας*, Athens 1982; V. Athanassopoulos, *Μεσσηνιακά Γράμματα* Β' (1967), p. 32-50.

For the period from 1204 to 1566, see W. Miller, *Ιστορία της Φραγκοκρατίας στην Ελλάδα*, Athens 1960. For the situation in the Peloponnese during the Byzantine period, see A. Bon, *Le Péloponnèse byzantin jusqu' à 1204*, Paris 1951; *idem*, Τα σύνορα των ενετικών κτήσεων εν Μεσσηνία από τον 13ο ως τον 15ο αιώνα, *Μεσσηνιακά Γράμματα* Β' (1967), p. 20-31. For the capture of Constantinople by the Franks, see Geoffrey Villehardouin, *The Conquest of Constantinople*, London 1829. For the Frankish period in the Peloponnese and topographical research based on the sources, see A. Bon, *La Morée franque*, Paris 1969; D. Zakynthinos, *Le Despotat grec de Morée 1262-1460*, Athens 1953.

For the Second Venetian period, see the collection of documents sent by Venice to her colonies of Methone and Corone in F. Thiriet, *Régestes des délibérations du Sénat de Venise concernant la Romanie*, Paris 1958-61; Th.D. Krimbas, Η ενετοκρατούμενη Πελοπόννησος, *Πελοποννησιακά* 1 (1956), p. 315-346 and 2 (1957), p. 247; A. Tselikas, Μεταφράσεις βενετικών εκθέσεων περί Πελοπονvήσου, *Πελοποννησιακά* 15 (1982-84), p. 127-152 and 21 (1995), p. 33-53; Ch. Maltezou, Οι πελοποννησιακές κτήσεις της Βενετίας, *IEE*, IX, p. 261-263; T. Gritsopoulos, Το εν Βενετία αρχείον Grimani καθ' όσον αφορά εις την Πελοπόννησον, *Πελοποννησιακά* 7 (1969-70), p. 396-399.

For the history and monuments of Venice, see G. Lorenzetti, *Venice and its Lagoon. Historical-Artistic Guide*, Trieste 1975.

For the second period of Turkish domination in the Peloponnese, see the seminal book by M. Sakellariou, *Η Πελοπόννησος κατά την δευτέραν Τουρκοκρατίαν*, Athens 1939.

For the evolution of fortress architecture from the Romans to the Byzantines, as revealed by defence works throughout the empire until 1261 and 1453, see A.W. Lawrence, A Skeletal History of Byzantine Fortification, *BSA* 78 (1983), p. 171-227. For the form taken by defence works during the Crusader period in the lands of the eastern Mediterranean, see W. Müller-Wiener, *Castles of the Crusaders*, New York - Toronto 1966; H. Kennedy, *Crusaders Castles*, 1994; A. Bon, Forteresses médiévales de la Grèce Centrale, *BCH* LXI (1937), p. 136-208, pl. XV-XXI; *idem*, Note additionnelle sur les forteresses médiévales de la Grèce Centrale, *BCH* LXII (1938), p. 441-442, which examines the fortresses and defence towers at Vodonitsa, Salona (Amphissa), Livadia and Thebes. For fortress architecture after the use of firearms became generalised, see the detailed study by I.Th. Steriotou, *Οι βενετικές οχυρώσεις του Ρεθύμνου (1540-1646). Συμβολή στη φρουριακή αρχιτεκτονική του 16ου και 17ου αιώνα*, *EpistEpetPolytThess* VII, Thessaloniki 1979; *eadem*, Ένας διάλογος σχετικά με την κατασκευή των φρουρίων (Fortezze), *EpistEpetPolytThess* VI, 2, Thessaloniki 1974, p. 99-174. For a concise description of Venetian architecture in Greece, see Ch. Bouras, *Αρχιτεκτονικά θέματα*, Athens 1970, p. 78; N. Moutsopoulos, *Πύργοι και κάστρα. Ερμηνευτικό λεξικό αρχαιοελληνικών στρατιωτικών όρων*, Athens 1972; N. Lianos, Μελέτη στα αρχαία λιμενικά έργα της Μεθώνης, *Αναστήλωση, Προστασία,* II, 1987, p. 129-135; Ch. Tzobanaki Οι χαμηλές πλατείες των προμαχώνων των βενετικών οχυρώσεων του Χάνδακα. Συμβολή στη μελέτη τους, *Αναστήλωση, Προστασία,* II, 1987, p. 105-128; D. Poziopoulos, Η μεταβατική μορφή των μεσαιωνικών οχυρώσεων της Ρόδου προς αντιμετώπιση των πυροβόλων όπλων, *Αναστήλωση, Προστασία,* I, 1984, p. 177-200. For fortresses in general, see *Πρακτικά της Η' Συνόδου του Διεθνούς Ινστιτούτου Φρουρίων και Πύργων*, 1968, p. 25-29; D. Zivas, Βενετσιάνικα κάστρα στην Ελλάδα, *Φρουριακά Χρονικά* 1 (1973), p. 109-125; E. Karpodini-Dimitriadi, *Κάστρα της Πελοποννήσου*, Athens 1993; A. Paradisis, *Φρούρια και κάστρα της Ελλάδος*, 2, Athens 1983; I.Th. Sfikopoulos, *Τα μεσαιωνικά κάστρα του Μοριά*, Athens 1968; Sl. Curcić - E. Hadjitryphonos, *Secular Medieval Architecture in the Balkans 1300-1500 and its Preservation*, Thessaloniki 1997.

For the battle of Lepanto, see V. Stavrogiannopoulos, *Ναυμαχία Ναυπάκτου μεταξύ χριστιανικού και οθωμανικού στόλου*, Athens 1972.

For the recapture of the Peloponnese by the Turks in 1715, see B. Brue, *Journal de la campagne que le grand Vézir a fait en 1715 pour la conquête de Morée,* Paris 1870 (reprint N. Karavia, Athens 1973).

For the Orloff episode, see S.V. Kougeas, Συμβολαί εις την ιστορίαν υπό τους Ορλώφ πελοποννησιακής επαναστάσεως (1770), *Πελοποννησιακά* 1 (1956), p. 50-107; T.A. Gritsopoulos, *Τα Ορλωφικά. Η εν Πελοποννήσω επανάστασις του 1770 και τα επακολουθήσαντα αυτής*, Athens 1967; S.V. Kougeas, Η καταγωγή του πρωτοστατήσαντος εις την ορλωφικήν επανάστασιν Παναγιώτη Μπενάκη, φωτιζομένη από τα αρχεία της Βενετίας, *Πελοποννησιακά* 6 (1963-1968), p. 1-42.

For the brig *Ares*, see *Μεγάλη Στρατιωτική και Ναυτική Εγκυκλοπαιδεία*, with an extract from the ship's diary. For General Maison, see V. Kremmydas, Ο γαλλικός στρατός στην Πελοπόννησο, *Πελοποννησιακά* 12 (1976-77), p. 75-102.

For the battle of Navarino, see C.M. Woodhouse, *The Battle of Navarino*, 1965; F. Michalopoulos, *Το Ναυαρίνον και η Ελληνική Επανάστασις*, Athens 1958; *IEE*, XII, p. 466-468, Sp. Loukatos, Η ναυμαχία του Ναβαρίνου, *Πρακτικά Γ' Διεθνούς Συνεδρίου Πελοποννησιακών Σπουδών*, p. 229-253. For the sole testimony from the side defeated in the battle, see G. Korinthios, Η ναυμαχία του Ναβαρίνου όπως την έζησε και την κατέγραψε ο G. Romey, *Πελοποννησιακά* 17 (1987-88), p. 117-142. See also the official Egyptian view of the battle in G. Douin, *Navarin (6 Juillet-20 Octobre 1827)*, Cairo 1927.

After the achievement of Greek independence, the first detailed account of the Pylia and its monuments, accompanied by detailed drawings, is that by the French expeditionary force under General Maison. The studies and drawings are contained in *Expédition Scientifique de Morée, ordonnée par le gouvernement français*. Architecture, I, Paris 1831-1838.

For Paliokastro and Niokastro and the castles of Messenia and the Peloponnese in general, see K. Andrews, *Castles of the Morea*, Princeton, NJ 1953, in which the drawings by the Venetian engineers now in the Gennadius Library are published; E. Forbes-Boyd, *In Crusader Greece*, London 1964. For Pylos and its history, see A.P. Michail, *Ιστορία της πόλεως Πύλου*, Athens 1888; G. Tarsouli,

Μεσσηνία, Πύλος, Athens n.p.d. Char. Baltas, *Η Πύλος από των αρχαιοτάτων χρόνων μέχρι των ημερών του Παυσανίου*, Athens 1968; *idem*, *Πύλος, Ναβαρίνο, Νιόκαστρο, Ανάκτορο Νέστορος*, Athens 1987; V.D. Kaldis, *Ταξίδι στην νεώτερη Πύλο*, Athens 1978; *idem*, *150 χρόνια από την εθνική μας αποκατάσταση*, Athens 1979, with a brief bibliography on Santa Rosa; T. Demodos, *Για το Νιόκαστρο και το Ναβαρίνο*, Athens 1987; *Η ιστορική Πύλος και ο Ολυμπιονίκης Κωστής Τσικλητήρας*, Athens 1960. For Philhellenism, see. L. Droulia, *Philhellénisme, ouvrages inspirés par la guerre de l'Indépendance grecque (1821-1833)*, Athens 1978. For the philhellene sentiments of Victor Hugo and his collection of poems *Les Orientales*, see R. Milliex, *Ελληνογαλλικά*, I, Athens 1953, p. 1-24.

For René Puaux and his collection, see G.S. Korres, Ο Puaux και η Πύλος, newspaper *Εστία*, 19-8-1978; R. Milliex, Ο ακάματος συμπαραστάτης του Ελληνισμού, προσφορά στην αγαπημένη του θετή πατρίδα, newspaper *Καθημερινή*, 11-1-1979. For his work, see Ang. Amandry, Η συλλογή René Puaux, *ΔΙΕΕ* 22 (1979), p. 38-62; *eadem*, *Η Ελληνική Επανάσταση σε γαλλικά κεραμικά του 19ου αιώνα*, Athens 1982; R. Puaux, *Le Philhellénisme. Collection René Puaux*, Catalogue de l'exposition, Paris 1936.

For Methone, see G. Soulis, Notes on Venetian Modon, *Πελοποννησιακά* 3-4 (1958-59), p. 267-275; N. Kotsiris, *Συμβολή στην ιστορία της Μεθώνης*, Athens 1983; S. Luce, Modon - A Venetian Station in Medieval Greece, *Classical and Medieval Studies in Honour of E.K. Rand*, New York 1938; F. Evangelatou-Notara, Η Μεθώνη, σταθμός στα ταξείδια βυζαντινών αυτοκρατόρων στην Δύση, *Πελοποννησιακά* 16 (1985-86), p. 97-107; V. Laurent, *Les «Mémoires» du Grand Ecclésiarque de l'Eglise de Constantinople Sylvestre Syropoulos*, Pontificum Institutum Orientalum Studiorum, Rome 1971; A. Momferatos, *Μεθώνη και Κορώνη επί Ενετοκρατίας υπό κοινωνικήν, πολιτικήν, δημοσιονομικήν έποψιν*, Athens 1914. For the shipwrecks in the sea of Methone, see P. Throckmorton, Underwater Surveys in Greece, *Expedition* 5, 2 (1963), p. 17-23; G. Papathanassopoulos, Έρευναι βυθού παρά την νήσον Σαπιέντζαν, *ADelt* 18 (1963), Chronika, p. 93.

For Corone, see F.K. Litsas, *Κορώνη, η προσωπογραφία μιας πολιτείας*, Athens 1983; I. Kakouris, Βυζαντινά γλυπτά της αρχαιολογικής Συλλογής Κορώνης, *Πελοποννησιακά* 12 (1978), p. 323-330; V. Marandos, *Κορώνη*, Athens 1976; D. Mourdoukoutas, *Κορώνη, ιστορικά-χριστιανικά μνημεία*, Messene 1952; K. Bebonis, *Κορώνης ιστορικαί σελίδες*, Athens 1906; A. Vassilikopoulou-Ioannidou, Η Επισκοπή Κορώνης στις αρχές του ιγ' αιώνα. Ο επίσκοπος Αθανάσιος, *Πελοποννησιακά* 16 (1985-86), p. 376-384; I. Demakopoulos, Η εκκλησία του Αγίου Ρόκκου στα Χανιά, *Εκκλησίες στην Ελλάδα μετά την Άλωση*, 1, Athens 1979, p. 257-267; C. Hodgetts, Land Problems in Coron 1298-1347, *Byzantina* 12 (1983), p. 135-157; M.I. Manousakas, Αρχιερείς Μεθώνης, Κορώνης και Μονεμβασίας γύρω στα 1500, *Πελοποννησιακά* 3-4 (1958-59), p. 95-147; G.S. Ploumidis, Συλλογή εγγράφων για τις βενετοκρατούμενες Μεθώνη και Κορώνη, *Πελοποννησιακά* 10 (1974), p. 155-164. For the policy of the European powers in the first half of the 16th c., see I.K. Chasiotis, Η Πελοπόννησος στο πλαίσιο της μεσογειακής πολιτικής του Καρόλου Ε', *Πελοποννησιακά* 15 (1982-84), p. 187-240. For the vernacular architecture of the settlements of Methone and Corone, see P. Grigorakis - S. Migaki - D. Charalambous, *Ελληνική παραδοσιακή αρχιτεκτονική. Πελοπόννησος*, 4, I, Athens 1985.

SOURCES OF ILLUSTRATIONS

ARCHAEOLOGICAL RECEIPTS FUND ARCHIVE
Cover illustration, 4, 6, 8, 23, 27, 31, 32, 34, 35, 41-44, 49, 77-80, 82-85, 87, 91-92, 95, 99-101, 140, 142, 146-148, 153, 158-160, 163, 165-166, 168-172, 178, 183, 185-188, 191, 193-194.

PHOTOGRAPHS BY THANOS PAPATHANASSOPOULOS
68, 86, 93-94, 128, 130-131, 137, 139, 150, 173γ, 182.

PHOTOGRAPHS BY LILY PAPATHANASSOPOULOU
3, 67, 125, 136, 141, 156.

GEORGE A. PAPATHANASSOPOULOS ARCHIVE
37, 132, 134, 175, 177.

V. KONSTANTAKOPOULOS ARCHIVE
5, 9, 64, 73.

GRIMANI COLLECTION
65-66, 75, 96, 143, 152, 184.

RENÉ PUAUX COLLECTION IN THE PYLOS ART GALLERY
61, 106, 109-111, 113, 116-118, 122, 123, 126, 135, 151.

1. Boissonas, 1905.
2. C. Bursian, *Geographie von Griechenland*, Leipzig 1871, pl. V.
7. K. Kourouniotis, Πύλου Μεσσηνιακής θολωτός τάφος, *AEphem* 1914, p. 108 and G. Korres, *Tropis* I, Athens 1989, σ. 200.
17. C.W. Blegen, Revealing the Palace of Homer's Nestor, *The Illustrated London News*, 16, 1 (1954).
18. *PN I, 2*, fig. 416.
19. *PN III*, fig. 303.
20. *PN II*, pl. M. Watercolour Piet de Jong.
21-22. *PN I, 2*. Watercolour Piet de Jong.
24. *PN II*, pl. O. Watercolour Piet de Jong.
25. *PN II*, pl. M. Watercolour Piet de Jong.
26. *PN I, 2*, fig. M.
28. Made available by Ch. Androutsakis.
29. *PN I, 2*, 378, no. 408.
30. *PN I, 2*, fig. 328.
36. C.W. Blegen, An Inscribed Tablet from Pylos, *AEphem* 1953-1954, p. 60.
38. *PN I, 2*, fig. 223.
39. *PN III*, fig. 221.
40. *PN III*, fig. 188.
45. G. Papathanassopoulos (based on the maps of W. McDonald - G.R. Rapp, Jr., *The Minnesota Messenia Expedition*, Minneapolis 1972.
46. Ancient Agora Museum.
48. Museo Nazionale di Napoli.
50-56. I. Ioannidou - L. Bartzioti.
58. Paris, Bibliothèque de l'Arsenal.
59. *Η Ιστορία της Βυζαντινής Αυτοκρατορίας*, University of Cambridge, Athens 1979, map 6.
60. Pylos Art Gallery. Donation of P.M. Melas.
62. *Views of Venice by Canaletto*, New York 1971, pl. XIV.
63. Giovanni Giacomo de Rossi, *Teatro della guerra contro il Turco*, Rome 1687.

70. Painting by the artist and engraver Pizanello (1380-1456).
71. Painting attributed to the great painter of the Cretan school Georgios Klontzas (16th-17th c.), Athens, National Historical Museum.
72. *ESM,* pl. 5.
74. Drawing by I. Baxevanakis, 1984.
76. *ESM,* pl. 2, fig. III.
88. G. Tarsouli, *Μεσσηνία, Πύλος*, Athens, n.p.d., fig. 92.
89. *ESM,* pl. 3, fig. 1, 2.
90. *ESM,* pl. 4.
98. Drawing by I. Baxevanakis - Th. Papathanassopoulos.
103. From *Λεξικόν το μέγα και πάνυ ωφέλιμον Βαρίνου Φαβωρίνου Κάρμητος*, Venice 1802.
104. Choiseul Gouffier, *Voyage pittoresque de la Grèce*, Brussels 1823.
105. Oil-painting by Thomas Phillips (1814). Collection of the British Embassy at Athens.
107. Oil-painting Peter Hess. Athens, National Historical Museum.
112. Gennadius Library.
114. Athens, National Historical Museum.
115. Oil-painting by the artist Polychronis Lembesis. Athens, National Historical Museum.
119. Gennadius Library.
120. G. Douin, *Navarin (6 Juillet-20 Octobre 1827)*, Cairo 1927.
121. Versailles Museum.
124. Paris, Bibliothèque Nationale.
127. Musée Langlois, Caen.
133. N. Valmin, *Det Underbara Grekland*, Stockholm 1939, p. 100.
138. Model by Elina Zenetou, 1984.
144. Centre of Modern Greek Research.
145. Boissonas, 1927.
149. K. Andrews, *Castles of the Morea*, Princeton, NJ 1953, p. 62, fig. 61.
154. *ESM,* pl. 14, fig. II.
155. Corfu. Venetian archives.
157. Ch. Bouras, Επανεξέταση του λεγομένου Αγιολέου κοντά στην Μεθώνη, *Φίλια Έπη εις Γ.Ε. Μυλωνάν*, III, 1989, p. 309, fig. 3 and 312, fig. 4.
161. K. Andrews, *Castles of the Morea*, Princeton NJ 1953, p. 69.
164. *ESM,* pl. 12, fig. II.
167. Ch. Bouras, *Αρχιτεκτονικά Θέματα,* 1970, p. 78.
173a. Greek National Archives (letter of Kapodistrias).
173b. Athens, National Historical Museum.
174, 176. P. Throckmorton, *Expedition* 5, 2 (1963), p. 17-23.
179-180. Fr. Versakis, Το Ιερόν του Απόλλωνος Κορύθου, *ADelt* 2 (1916), p. 77 and 71.
190. G. Tarsouli, *Μεσσηνία, Πύλος*, Athens, n.p.d., fig. 75.
195. *ESM,* pl. 17, fig. I.
196. Boissonas, 1905.

The drawings and maps are by G. Papathanassopoulos with the exception of those for which a different source is cited.

South-west Peloponnese

● *Main towns and villages*